SACRAMENTS AND PASSAGES

Celebrating the Tensions of Modern Life

GERARD FOUREZ, SJ

Ave Maria Press
Notre Dame, Indiana

265
Fo 5

Imprimi Potest: J. M. Hennaux, SJ
                  Provincial, Province of South Belgium
                  1981

International Standard Book Number: 0-87793-301-4

Library of Congress Catalog Card Number: 83-71164

Printed and bound in the United States of America.

Cover and text design: Elizabeth French

Contents

About the Author

Gerard Fourez is a professor at the University of Namur in Belgium where he concentrates on issues related to ethics and religion in modern society. He is also a visiting professor in the summer at La Salle College in Philadelphia.

He is the author of a number of books, including *I Believe in God . . . What Do I Honestly Believe?* (Dimension, 1982) and *Liberation Ethics* (Temple University Press, 1982). His writings have also appeared in *Chicago Studies, US Catholic, The Catholic World, Sisters Today, Review for Religious, The Priest, Nuclear Physics* and *Physical Review.* A native of Belgium, Father Fourez graduated from the University of Louvain, holds advanced degrees from Woodstock College and earned a Ph.D. at the University of Maryland.

Acknowledgments

I want to thank all those who have helped me with their remarks, criticism, and suggestions: my students, my colleagues, and my friends. Among many I want to mention are B. Hogan who edited the English translation and gave many useful suggestions; also M. F. Becker, V. Beuvens, P. De Clerck, D. Dufrasne, C. Gortebecke, M. Ivereigh, A. Postal, B. Radtke, G. Rulmont-Ugeux, S. Séron, and P. Tihon.

I want to mention the secretarial help of J. Cratin, N. Renkin, and C. Fallay; the support of my University in Belgium (Facultés N.D. de la Paix, Namur) and of La Salle College (Philadelphia); the concern of Mr. Frank Cunningham, editor of Ave Maria Press, and of Mr. Charles Ehlinger, editor of Le Centurion Press (Paris).

Preface

The sacraments today seem to be in captivity; their power is not easily revealed in a technological society which is out of step with rites and with symbolic language. Our society prefers rational discourse and univocal processes.

In this book I would like to contribute to the restoration of the sacraments as celebrations that have real meaning in the lives of Christians today. I do not intend to submit a normative theory of rites or a complete theology of Christian sacraments. Nor do I attempt to relate the book to the classical understanding of the sacraments in the context of tradition and scripture—which may in fact be the starting point of many readers.

My starting point is communities that celebrate rites, sometimes sacramental rites, sometimes non-sacramental rites. This book presents a theory only insofar as it systematically describes what is already experienced by groups. It thus starts from actual living traditions and not from theology.

Consequently, I do not try to reflect on all the wealth of Christian traditions related to sacraments. My aim is narrower. It assumes one way, among several other ways, to practice theology, that method which starts with the living faith of the communities and which has sometimes been called "inductive theology."

The method I choose can raise questions that I will briefly discuss in this preface. The reader less interested in these methodological matters can skip these pages which are more technical and difficult than the rest of the book.

The inductive method has the advantage of being directly in touch with what is experienced by groups and by grassroot communities. It has the disadvantage, inherent in any specific spirituality, of giving more emphasis to some aspects of the traditions than to others. It would be unfair to assume, however, that those who practice such a method are denying what they do not make explicit. That rule is, moreover, valid for any kind of theological work. No theology can claim a complete overview of Christian revelation.

This kind of inductive theology is not as new as some people think. It could even be shown that it was the usual method of theological thought, all of which must in the final analysis stem from the living experience of Christian communities. (I do not speak here of theological textbooks which are simply summaries of the results of theological reflection through the centuries.) In particular, sacramental theology has never been, for the Fathers of the church, anything other than a systematic explanation of the *lex orandi*, the concrete way the people of God were celebrating and praying. It is in that spirit that, from the ninth to the 13th centuries, the so-called *questiones* and *determinationes* were elaborated. It is only from the 16th century that for many reasons, including the rise of a new scientific rationality, a new theological method, deductive and rationalistic, took over.

In this book I intend to use symbolic language in its typical spontaneity, refusing the positivistic approach which reduces everything to its rational dimension. The quotations of the gospel have to be understood in that context; to quote the gospel without demythologizing it does not mean that I want to belittle all that modern exegesis has produced. The same principle applies to the use of ritual languages; their meaning is derived from reference to the experiences of living communities. A purely rationalist way of looking at ritual language is definitely too limited.

Some will perhaps say that this book places too much

emphasis on what happens in the community and not enough on the direct action of God. This emphasis will puzzle only those who are not used to recognizing God and his action through what is human. This book presupposes that God becomes visible *through the human reality* of actions and rituals and not beside them. To affirm that it is the rite itself that is effective does not belittle the action of God. A rite is simply a way to make clearer how God acts among men and women. This is important if we want to avoid the typical false dilemma expressed in the following questions: Is Christian faith vertical or horizontal? Is it transcendent or immanent?

This book could be entitled "The Sacraments Viewed Through Phenomenology and Sociology." At first sight it could easily appear as a sociological study of the sacraments. A purely sociological reading will see rites as social devices for coping with social tensions, but not as manifestations or revelations of God. But sacraments are not first a tool for the church to use in handling social conflict. They are primarily celebrations where, in faith, Christians recognize Christ as the heart and the source of every liturgy; he appears as the one who reconciles human beings with one another and with God.

Some, depending on their specific spirituality, will be more in tune with images of Christ which show his transcendence and with the impossibility of identifying completely the Christ manifested in human images. They will rather speak of the Lord of the world, of the master of truth, of the one who is united with the church and offers it to the Father, etc. My tendency is rather to seek Christ who is committed to the entire human experience through the historical wandering of the people of God in salvation history. If I stress the human reality celebrated in our liturgies, I do not intend to reduce the sacraments to a celebration by Christians of their own life, excluding God. But I believe that the liturgy can help to celebrate Christ, the gift of God, who manifests himself *in* the entire history of men and women, and not just on certain occasions in human history.

These two kinds of spirituality have each their advantages and problems. They probably have some of that complementarity which is so necessary to Christian communities. What is important is, on the one hand, to be sure that openness to the manifestation of God in history does not end by being completely immersed in history, to the point of becoming unable to receive and to express symbolically the gratuitous gift of God. In other words, I want to stress that worship—even with some of the ambiguities this term can conceal—is a constitutive dimension of Christian traditions. But, on the other hand, that dimension should not hide the reality that, according to the same traditions, it is through history that God becomes visible, making of human history the very history of salvation and of liberation for men and women.

A complete exposition of the methodology of this book, which uses social sciences as well as theology, would require some theoretical developments that I will not present here. This methodology raises issues that are traditional, at least from the time that the Middle Ages began questioning the relationship of theology and philosophy. (Philosophy had, at that time, a similar function to the one fulfilled today by social sciences.) Is theology a social science? If so, what is its specificity? What is the relationship between theology and faith? How can social sciences address the topics that theology treats? What are the relationships between the following: expressions of faith, scholarly theologies, and analyses of Christian commitment by social sciences? These issues refer to the faith commitment that underlies theological rationality, as well as to the specific ideologies which are at the foundation of social sciences and other academic disciplines. They also refer to questions relative to the very nature of rationality. These problems have no simple solutions in our day.

Theological method is often defined as the interpretation of the scriptures within the living traditions of the church. With such a definition theology would seem to be able to work without any help from social sciences. However, from the Middle Ages on, it has been accepted that theology always presupposes and uses a philosophy. The definition of theology would indeed be more appropriate if people would add, following in that the guidelines of Vatican II: ". . . in the living traditions of the church *facing the world*." In such a framework it becomes obvious that theology requires some outside perspective that, through its intrusions, challenges the theologians when they become too satisfied with their way of expressing the faith and of understanding it. Thus social sciences do not simply give some results that theology then uses, as if they were ideologically neutral; rather, social sciences bring to theology a confrontation necessary so that it does not get ossified and far away from the "world."

The present book thus stems from the life of Christian communities who confront their faith practices with the way disciplines such as phenomenology, sociology, political and economic analysis, look at them. These disciplines, however, do not have an epistemological status according to which they can objectively judge Christian faith. They are, just as theology is, connected to particular practices and to concrete solidarities. But social sciences—in the manner of the pagans in St. Paul—force people to have a renewed look at faith, and, in our specific case, at the sacraments. The relationship of these faith realities with the salvific event—Jesus—is then perceived in a new light, and some aspects of sacramental life begin to be clearer. Finally, in a further step, what is thus articulated as a possible theological thesis, has to be confronted with the scriptures, interpreted within the living traditions of the church. This confrontation is always incomplete because it cannot be merely theoretical. It is the whole people of God—and not only the scholars or even the bishops—who can articulate norms for Christian faith.

This approach shows that there are important issues related to theological rationality in Christian communities. How is it possible to link, in a correct dialectic relationship, a double expression of Christian faith: the spontaneous expression of the people and the intellectual one of clerical theologians (even if these theologians may sometimes be lay persons in the canonical meaning of the term)? How can the church deal with this already very old social differentiation of roles in the Christian community: the people (the "laos" or lay persons) and the clerics ("those who can read")? These issues have repercussions on rituals and sacraments. On the one hand, people want to celebrate their life, while on the other hand a clerical class always recalls—as its proper function and ministry—that it is not true that any kind of rite can celebrate Jesus Christ. Such a social organization institutes some dialectic tensions that are too often concealed or not addressed by theories that legitimate, and sometimes very well, the magisterium.

Some of the tensions between popularized religion and theological rationality are in the background of this book. To reduce these tensions to some superficial dysfunction of present Christian ministries—the ministry of the magisterium and the ministry of theology, especially—would not reach the heart of the issue. Similarly, the question goes far beyond some anticlerical aggressiveness—somewhat understandable—with respect to the establishment. Beyond all that, what is at stake is, in my opinion, the violence inherent in any kind of rationality, whether it be called scientific or theological. More research is needed on the theological and social implications of the double Christian discourse: the spontaneous expression of the faith and the "learned" theological discourse. Theoretical analyses of that dialectic will probably show that concepts of orthodoxy and of theological truth and methods are not as clear as a superficial view might imply. Analysis could give insights into the social roots of these concepts and into the important ministry traditionally called "magisterium."

The aim of this book is not to clarify these theoretical issues which are part of the complex area where faith and social sciences dialogue. It is, rather, addressed to a technological society in which overly rationalistic thought categories tend to stifle nearly every kind of celebration. Its aim is to provide some space for the sacraments to be and to act on society, with all the power of their dynamics.

—GERARD FOUREZ, SJ

1 | Rites and Sacraments in Modern Society

Our society, centered on output and efficiency, sometimes leaves little room for celebration. Human beings take less and less time to celebrate, wrapped up as they are in carrying out programs which the daily grind imposes upon them. Symbols, rites and rituals are thus neglected. As the fox sadly laments in Saint-Exupéry's *The Little Prince,* these humanizing events are often forgotten; men and women no longer have time to get in touch with their lives, things and people.

Almost all rites are affected by this crisis but in different ways. It is not easy to analyze the crisis and its causes. The Eucharist, for example, still attracts people to it, but most of the other sacraments are somewhat neglected or are in difficulty. A funeral still appears to be one of the Christian occasions that best meets the needs of the people, but it just happens that this rite is not recognized as a sacrament. Some communities try to live without bothering about sacramental theology. On the other hand, it seems that as soon as "sacraments" come on the scene, a concern for orthodoxy often breaks spontaneity. Might this not be one of the reasons why the sacraments do not work well? What causes a rite to meet or fail to meet people's expectations?

Beyond the rational:
rites as expressions of the tensions of existence

In this work I shall consider rites as symbolic acts and

celebrations which mark a significant moment. I am not concerned with stereotyped and repetitive gestures—rites of daily life—which, although reducing anxiety, possess scarcely any symbolic echoes.

Rites are present in all cultures; their chief role seems to be to help human beings get in touch with events and "passages" in existence which resist the cold and univocal language of reason. Lying at the center of religious traditions, and of Christian traditions in particular, rites go beyond rational and moralizing arguments; they open the way to depths of loving which can be felt only through ritual.

My basic assumption is that in every human society, whenever an event of any importance occurs, people use rites in order to live it. This is true even in our society which has lost many of its traditional rites. Unfortunately, it has replaced them with a technical mind-set which seeks immediate answers to all questions in order to "tame" the realities of life. This mind-set expresses itself in a language in which there is one and only one word for each thing, and therefore the answers it proposes are inadequate; they suit only what Marcuse has called a "one-dimensional society."

Rites always relate to tensions of existence: What is solely factual is not the object of a rite. An existential tension, however, whether it is lived or is being resolved, cannot be conveyed by a language that is only rational or factual; it demands a ritual. If I want to convey my sympathy to someone who has recently been bereaved, the content of what I say will always be inadequate or will sound false; but the ritual gesture of putting my hand on that person's shoulder can convey my affection and sympathy; it enables me to get in touch with the tension experienced, to act it out and to express it. The same applies to a funeral. There is a set of rites that accompany the confrontation with someone's death and the ensuing restructuring of life and social relationships. In nearly all cultures, celebrations also mark the end of an important task, such as the harvest. Relaxation, joy and gratitude for what has been accomplished are conducive to celebration, as a shared common experience. Rites likewise mark departures, comings of age, marriage, birth, decisions, the end of school education, the appointment of a leader, retirement, and so on. What characterizes each of these events is an experienced tension linked to social relationships which assume new forms and structures.

Nearly all these tensions are part of conflicts. While a marriage is an occasion for joy, it also entails risks and will lead to conflicts. These conflicts will perhaps arise in the married couple, between the spouses and their families, or among these families, or in connection with work obligations. The birth of a child likewise changes the life of the parents and their social relationships. Other obligations arise, a new negotiation of the relationships between husband, wife and the various children will follow; this does not always take place smoothly. The same applies to almost all situations in which human beings use rites; they involve joy, pains, tensions and conflicts.

My hypothesis is therefore, on the one hand, that the sacraments are linked to individual or collective transitions and to tensions of existence and society, and on the other hand, that sacramental celebrations become insipid and pointless when they are seen without reference to those tensions, transitions or conflicts. Furthermore, when these tensions are taken into account, the meaning of the sacraments is illuminated and the rites help people to get in touch with the human realities to which they refer.

Rites thus concern the most profound tensions of existence; they always call to mind its ultimate dimensions: the transcendent in one form or another. Rites do not speak only of what one does or what one has; in the face of the critical moments of existence they refer to what one ultimately *is*. That is why they nearly always involve the religious dimension. In the face of the "passages" which they call to mind, the truth of everything relating to living is at stake. This explains why they represent one of those privileged places where God becomes manifest and where human beings come face to face with God. The ritual expressions of these passages of God (Pasch) are thus, very naturally, one of the principal bases of prayer and worship.

The effectiveness of celebrations

The distinctive nature of ritual celebration is to enable the tensions the rites evoke to be lived in a better way; in this sense, a good rite is always effective in itself. In theological language, this means that sacramental grace is not something which follows the rite or which comes with it; grace is effected by the celebration itself, which, in helping people to live the transition celebrated, becomes a manifestation of God's love. The effectiveness of rites can be noted in highly varied circumstances. For example, if someone leaves on a long journey, a farewell party is given. This party and its preparation will make it possible to live the separation, to get used gradually to the idea of departure, and to experience this transition in a human fashion. A good farewell party is not a magic rite; it achieves something. After the farewell party a person is no longer the same and does not approach the separation in the same way; its rites have restructured social relationships.

The Quakers have a marvelous expression for describing the action of a celebration when they say that it has "spoken to their condition." Likewise, one comes back from some funerals saying, "That has done me good; I'm now more ready to face the future." The same happens after a properly celebrated marriage; parents accept with greater peace the fact that their child is now following his or her own road and does not need them anymore. Here, again, the ritual celebration has made it possible to live a change in social relationships, to get in touch with it, and to "tame" the new reality that must be lived.

Beyond univocal language

Tackling the study of rites from this viewpoint obviously involves dissociating oneself from the set forms in which a rationalist theology had in the past enclosed sacramental rites. Too often the leading place given to theology or to reason rather than to what is lived by Christians and their communities animated by the breath of the Spirit has resulted in static rituals. The aim then is solely to do what is enjoined by an abstract norm. In fact, norm and tradition are thereby confused with each other. We know, however, that a tradition is a whole past which enables new meanings to be discerned, while a norm is liable to imprison meaning in its rationality. As soon as an important event is experienced, reason (at least linear, one-dimensional, deductive reason) is no longer sufficient. In the face of straightforward situations—asking someone for directions—reason works very well; there are no problems. In more complex circumstances, however, language no longer works in the same way; words become insufficient and empty. At such a moment, ritual gestures are used almost automatically. The way in which these gestures operate is very significant; they must not say too much, but they must bear a meaning that has been given to them beforehand by a cultural tradition. Thus, if I put my hand on the shoulder of a sufferer, this gesture may function as a rite; it saves me from spelling out my feelings in words which would fall flat. As this gesture is known in our culture, the person concerned realizes that I am trying to say something like, "I am with you." Without a cultural tradition which already gives it a certain meaning, that person would wonder what was happening. Thanks to this tradition, the gesture becomes word, but a word which does not exhaust everything of which the gesture is a bearer. At the same time communication is not lost in a univocal formula which would be out of place in such circumstances.

A pluri-vocal language

A rite is therefore predetermined by a culture but, contrary to rational or scientific language, its significance remains open to several meanings. For the gesture or ritual celebration to assume its full dimension, the actors must themselves contribute. In the rite, however, one is not expected to say everything or to stick rigidly to what one says. This is the way the birthday cake ritual works. It symbolizes relationships, it says something, it is the basis of a bond between the persons concerned; but its meaning remains open, not fixed once and for all.

The central elements of rites are generally objects and gestures, but sometimes ritualized words as well. A striking example is the expression often repeated by lovers: "I love you." This expression is a rite, for it has no very specific rational substance (it can mean anything), although the cultural context more or less indicates the sense. Lovers can repeat these words to each other, for they do not confine the love relationship in a univocal language; the words express a relationship which is known to be inexpressible.

Into the ambiguity and multiple meanings of the rite everyone can put more or less what is desired. The words, "I love you," may be either empty or significant. The same goes for a birthday cake. Without the custom of baking a cake and singing a sort of all-purpose song, we might not know how to mark the occasion of someone's progress in life. It is important for the song to be rather general in nature. If it were too explicit it could not function as a rite and convey the sometimes differing or even ambiguous feelings of the participants. It is this imprecision which, in certain circumstances, can cause a rite to become a parody. It can express many meanings, but it cannot convey just anything without being actually distorted, or, to use religious vocabulary, sacrilegious. Such would be the case with a birthday celebration in a family where the dominant feeling is one of hatred.

A rite may therefore be perverted when, as indicated by the word's etymology, its meanings are distorted in order to introduce something quite different from what it is supposed to express. Such distortions may be intentional, for example in saying, "I love you," to someone whom one is betraying (the kiss of Judas), but most of the time the aberration operates through vague and unconscious social mechanisms. For instance, perversion occurs if baptism becomes an expression of the church's grip on the new member, rather than an expression of the liberation[1] of

1. In this book the term "liberation" is often preferred to the term "freedom" so as to express the biblical concept that speaks of people being freed slowly through holy history from slavery and sin. The concept of freedom too often evokes in our culture a kind of static state as if people were free once and for all. Such an understanding would be difficult to reconcile with the history of salvation.

which the original rite speaks. All the sacraments may be perverted when they cease to be the liberating power of God in order to become a means of "moralizing" and hence of controlling Christians, and sometimes even of setting traps for them.

To summarize what has just been said, a rite may be defined as a gesture or word having a meaning which is partly predetermined by the surrounding culture but which, at the same time, does not say too much, so that individuals or communities can get in touch with what is relevant to them while expressing a variety of meanings.

The myth of spontaneity

If this is true, everything claiming to be a spontaneous rite must be looked at cautiously. In fact, no completely spontaneous and new rite ever exists; what is lived is expressed through the characteristics of a culture. A new ritual may sometimes be created by putting together significant gestures which were not always brought together in the same way. But if someone were to institute a rite out of nothing, his or her behavior would simply appear strange; the person would probably be looked on as insane. Rites are not invented, any more than a language is invented; a rite is learned, and then it is enriched or transformed, but it is not created out of nothing. The construction of new rites is a slow process involving the whole progression of a community and requiring great energy. A celebration constructed in an almost entirely new manner, with no link with existing ritual structures, would be tiring and overly dependent on reasoning; at each moment it would be necessary to explain everything. When some people nonetheless try to create completely new rites, they often manage to design celebrations which speak more to the head than to the whole human being. On the other hand, real spontaneity becomes possible in communities sharing one and the same cultural root system; they succeed in expressing themselves thanks to fragments of rites known beforehand. They carry out a sort of do-it-yourself ritual by using a heritage of significant common characteristics.

This use of cultural elements already present is important in rites, all the more so because it is ritual that enables human beings to live through difficult moments without excessive fear and to master the passages of existence. Let us recall the meeting of the little prince and the fox in Saint-Exupéry's book. It is only by advancing little by little, a bit more each day, that the fox can be tamed, that is, will cease to be afraid of the little prince. There is a whole game in this, following which the anxiety-producing situation becomes acceptable: the game of coming closer. "It is a rite," says the fox as he invites the little prince to come gradually nearer. The repetitiveness of the rite is essential to its operation; it enables tension in the face of the unknown to be reduced. A rite is basically a "game" which acts out a transition; it helps one to become gradually used to reality. By familiarizing oneself with the new social relationships acted out in the rite, one learns gradually to accept them. The repetition is a way of saying and re-saying what cannot be expressed in logical language alone. Thus, when a marriage celebration is well-performed and prepared, a game of becoming aware of various feelings is played. This awareness process serves for the restructuring of the social relationships linked to marriage. The ritual repetition reduces tension and permits the necessary transitions. After all, this marriage is perhaps unique but there have been others before it, and there will be others after it which will be celebrated with similar words and gestures. Becoming aware that there is something common in this experience enables one to relax and to get in touch with what is being lived.

Development of the meaning of rites

In all cultures there are a number of established rites. These rites mark fairly important transitions in life in the face of which the community invites its members to get in touch with what is happening through a celebration. In the Western Latin world, the transitions which seem to have received the most importance are linked with the seven sacraments: welcoming a new member, recognizing that member as having his or her own voice in matters, asking for and granting forgiveness, facing decisions involving life and death, entering into the institution of marriage, commissioning a community leader, and finally living the moment for approaching the unknown. But these sacraments are not the only ritual celebrations of Catholics. I have already mentioned funerals. Let us consider Lent with its celebration of fasting, ashes and other symbols. Such celebrations—like all rites, in fact—may have a multitude of meanings. I shall examine some of them.

As expressed in all periods of history by the texts of the liturgy, the celebration of Lent is a way of marking the occasion with respect to the injustices of the world. The symbolic significance of fasting is doubtless connected with our psychobiology; there are situations which take away the appetite. To fast is to imitate losing our appetites, so as to familiarize ourselves with what, in our world, "takes away the appetite." The symbol of ashes revolves around similar meanings; at times of great dramas, one does not always take time to wash. One gets dirty as if covered with ashes. To live like this, moreover, is to be a deviant in society and to distance oneself from "those who live in palaces" (Mt 11:8). Further, when we are preoccupied with something of great importance, by some issue encompassing at a certain moment the whole of existence, we scarcely have time to eat. The ritual celebration of Lent leads those who devote themselves to it to act out, to relive all this and thereby to familiarize themselves with the realization that there exist situations in the world which are so serious that they genuinely take away the appetite, that one ceases to have time to wash, and that one is in the presence of evil. It is a feast of *distance* with respect to an unjust order, a distance which is felt with difficulty by those who never pause in the face of the consumer society. This feast also uses many other symbolic systems and intertwines with them: the acting out of the long march of liberation in the desert, hunger for the word of God, etc. These systems of symbols cannot be reduced to a single meaning.

Lent illustrates two important conditions for any community rite: traditions and developments. On the one hand, if people practice a "feast of distance," it is because tradition invites them to do so. Without this invitation, would we so easily allow ourselves to confront the conflicts underlying the fact of living in unjust societies? The invitation to ritual celebrations helps us to get in touch with conflicts, tensions and transitions which we would otherwise try to avoid. It is a call to live existence deeply and seriously.

On the other hand, the example of Lent indicates that the meanings of rites are ceaselessly refashioned. Those I have presented do not correspond exactly to another traditional conception of Lent linked to mortification. It is normal for the meanings of rites to evolve, since ritual symbols have a multiplicity of meanings and always go beyond the meanings which may be assigned to them by theoreticians. Being a symbol, the rite receives its meaning only when related to the whole context in which it is celebrated. It would therefore be futile to try to fix this meaning once and for all. It evolves in accordance with situations and cultures.

The transition from one meaning to another (which does not exclude the first because rites are plurisignificant) is sometimes called a "transaction." It consists in placing in the foreground a symbolic element which has previously been neglected. A transaction is often the stake in societal tensions and struggles. For instance, the celebration of Lent, as described above, resonates with the feelings of communities which are conscious of social injustices while, previously, Lent was more linked with a bourgeois society which was keen on calculating and saving and which accordingly assigned a very large place to asceticism lived for its own sake. That is why the most common presentations of Lent in the first half of the 20th century stressed asceticism and mortification; today, the emphasis seems to be on the theme of justice.

All rites—the sacraments included—are in this way the risk involved in ideological struggles; they reflect and seek to strengthen—or even to bring about—different social orders. Certain meanings of rites will be seen by some as perversions; this depends on the idea one has of a good society, of good social relationships, and finally of one's loyalties.

In our technological society many rites work badly. Communities have difficulty in comforting individuals when they are going through certain changes. They seem to have lost the capacity to symbolize the commitments which give the community its very foundation. In fact, in the hyperindustrialized world, rites have been replaced by managers and psychologists. Thus, at the moment of restructuring social relations, of living a transition, people tend to consult psychologists to help them take the step in question. In a more collective situation, a management expert will usually be called. In any case, the process is clear; science and technology have often taken over roles which ritual celebrations fulfill in other civilizations.

Rites and social relationships

In the background of rites loom social relationships. Whenever something is celebrated by a rite, social relations are formed and dissolved. Therefore societies, communities and individuals institute ritual celebrations in order to "tame" the tensions and conflicts linked to these social relationships. The rite is always a way of warding off the possible violence of social life, either by acting out the resolution of tensions or by celebrating their end, but in any event by living, feeling and symbolizing them. Celebrations which do not evoke and symbolize the conflicts and tensions of existence are quickly swallowed up in the banal and the insipid; they often become static and boring. This happens frequently, as dominant groups in society generally have an interest in seeing that little reference is made to societal tensions. The dominant ideology tends to produce ritual celebrations which incorporate the population into the "great harmony" that the dominant social order claims exists. The sacraments have not escaped this sociological law.

In order to understand celebrations, it is therefore necessary to examine social relationships and their underlying conflicts. In some cases, they are quite visible, as in the case of the sacrament of forgiveness, celebrations of departures, welcoming of a new member into the community, etc. But in other cases, they are apt to be veiled. For instance, many consider that a marriage celebration should speak only of the marvelous ideal; but such an unreal vision hides other aspects of actual experience: the family separations implied in the creation of the new couple, the ties of friendship and previous social commitments which will have to be structured differently, the conflicts which will be encountered by the couple. Likewise, the sacrament of ordination celebrates the hope that the new leaders of the Christian community will truly be signs of God's love for the people; however, one is also aware of the misdeeds of clericalism and of the virtual impossibility for human beings to institute a power which does not lead to abuses. By thus examining all the rites of a society, one would eventually see that they retain their depth only insofar as they do not conceal the social violence and tensions linked to what they celebrate. It is only when a celebration goes so far as to touch the contradictions present in individuals and communities that one leaves it "comforted." If the Pharisee in the parable returns home without having anything happen in his prayer it is precisely because, unlike the publican, he has not gotten in touch with the contradictions of his existence. However, not all the tensions celebrated by rites have to do with conflict. Even beyond conflicts, the depth of a celebration remains linked to existential tensions. Thus, the sacrament of the sick or the funeral rite will have consistency and will "speak to the condition of the people" only if these rites help them face the reality of disease and death, with all the unknown factors, all the questioning, all the separations which the two phenomena imply.

As celebrations are linked to social relationships and modifications in them, they have also to express the fears that accompany important passages in existence. The community which celebrates seeks to get in touch with the new situation and for that a whole social game is necessary; one says it, imagines it, denies it, acts it out, in short one prepares for it. To understand this "ritual game" it is sufficient to recall the way in which we tell someone that he or she is suffering from an incurable illness; we take our time in order that the person may, little by little, face up to what is happening and confront the tensions which it involves.

This approach to contradictions which are either social or individual is found in all rites, at least where they are not transformed into pure commercialized folklore. The celebration of Mardi gras is typical in this respect; while for some spectators it is only a show, for the actors—in the New Orleans event, at least—it is a profound rite. They save the whole year in order to take part in this celebration in which society's barriers and contradictions briefly melt away. At Mardi gras, hereditary enemies go so far as to embrace one another, and this does not ring false. Employers and employees may meet in the celebration; the usual barriers are transgressed. The celebration speaks of another world, of ways of living other than those one experiences daily. Its interest lies precisely in its break with the daily round. Christian theology will express this aspect of things when it speaks of an eschatological dimension of the sacraments, that is, the bursting into daily life of what otherwise exists only as a utopian aspiration.

What is lived in Mardi gras is also found in other rites, such as birthdays, which also mark a break with daily routine, in which people may find in one another something over and above what ordinarily divides them. The same applies to the celebration of a marriage; on such an occasion one speaks of the hope of shared life, full of tenderness and support, despite all the tensions present in the family institution.

Rites and social transgressions

Rites often function as points of no return, as transgressions in the etymological sense of the word (i.e., as the crossing of a frontier). Thus, sharing bread with an enemy may help to alter the relationship fundamentally; it is possible—and, in many cases, even probable—that there will be no reconciliation; but after the celebration one can no longer regard the other in exactly the same way.

Likewise, a celebration in which parents find themselves having to take seriously the fact that their child has received the Spirit of God and that this Spirit speaks in the child may profoundly modify the parent-child relationship. Rites therefore change something in existence to a point where it is no longer possible to go backwards; they create new social relationships. This is doubtless what has given rise to the magical conception of the rite; when, after a properly lived ritual celebration, we consider all that has happened, we sometimes have the impression of the waving of a magic wand.

Thus, well-performed rites break boundaries and lead people and groups to the frontiers of their existence—frontiers of which in some cases they were ignorant. They produce profound effects which are often as effective as psychotherapy. If they have this power, is it any wonder that a sacred dimension is normally attributed to them? Those, for example, who take part in a genuine Mardi gras know very well that something is going to happen and that they will not leave it as they entered it. The same applies to any celebration touching the depths of the human being and of society. One goes to it with the sort of fascination and apprehension which mark the approach to the sacred. One goes to it as Moses went to Sinai, knowing that he was going to encounter Yahweh. In properly lived rites, one may be compelled, either individually or collectively, to find oneself changed or to take a new step in life. How many people say to themselves with emotion, after a marriage, a retirement celebration, a funeral, a first communion, a workers' demonstration, "I was really moved by it and my/our existence has been transformed."

The example of a demonstration for a cause or a workers' strike is illuminating, because they can be regarded as rites. They *are* rites. They are not limited to the level of a strategy. All those who have taken part in one know that there is more to it than the action itself; through demonstrations, marches, strikes, people become aware of what they are living in society. It is through such celebrations for instance that black people—or opponents of the Vietnam war—became aware of the social relationships in which they were involved, as well as of the changes they wished to make in them. To decide to demonstrate is to enter a ritual action which possesses its distinctive effectiveness and thus contributes to changing the picture one forms of social relationships. These collective actions act partly independently of views of the leaders, as if by themselves, by a sort of *ex opere operato,* if such a comparison with classical theology may be ventured.

Traditions and passages

Most cultures supply communal aid at difficult times when one is embarking on the unknown and when social relationships are modified. From an anthropological viewpoint, situations such as those created by our industrial culture, which for example sometimes lets people die completely alone, are rare in human history. Generally, as soon as there is a change and transition to be lived—the proximity of death, coming of age, entering school or marriage, the appointment of a new leader, the emergence of social conflicts, the taking of important decisions—societies offer their members rites to enable them to tackle these traditions.

The rites offered by societies result from traditions. To live in a culture is to possess a number of ritual traditions on which individuals and communities draw according to their needs. Think of Christmas, Thanksgiving and Independence Day, for example. These traditions are generally linked to accounts of events associated with processes of foundation; such events indicate passages which will have to be faced. Thus, in the Christian liturgy, the eucharistic rite refers, on the one hand, to the "passing" of Yahweh who liberated the Hebrew people from Egypt and, on the other hand, to the "passing" of Jesus toward his death following his decision to experience to the end the conflict between him and the Pharisees and high priests. Through the hearing of such accounts, the eucharistic rite commemorates these founding events and thereby helps the participants to get in touch with those passages which are theirs. In theological language, they enter into the mystery of the death and resurrection of Jesus.

One could mention a host of similar examples. Marriage celebrations, for instance, generally make reference to traditional stories of love, which are in the nature of paradigms enabling people to get in touch with the new situation; in Christian traditions the story of God's love for his people is recalled. Even at birthday parties one hears family stories of the past. In cases where the original founding account has practically disappeared (as in the case of Mardi gras), the way is paved for the new celebration by stories of past celebrations and their effects.

Rites in a technical society

A malaise appears when social groups or individuals are no longer comfortable within their ritual traditions. There may be various reasons for this. For example, the working class in Europe lost confidence in the sacraments because these had often become means of integrating them into a social order which exploited them. But the more or less general discredit into which most of the sacraments and traditional ritual practices have fallen probably has its source elsewhere, in the very structures of industrial society. Technological efficiency and the one-dimensional scientific reasoning associated with it do not encourage ritual and symbolic languages.

The modification which has most influenced our society is probably the difference, on the one hand, between work-related and private-life-related roles and, on the other hand, between places of work and places of living. In a society where people worked where they lived, celebrations could be all-embracing; the same celebration covered what had been lived both in work and in personal relations. Thus, the celebration which followed the harvest sprang up very naturally after the tensions of work. The grain piled high in the barn was able to be a symbol of the work, relationships and success of the whole community; the celebration joined it all together. Likewise, Lent, Christmas or Easter brought together the local community, in all its dimensions. But today, even if Christmas is celebrated at work, this celebration touches only a very small part of existence. Industrial society has separated private life from work relationships. Where roles have been cut into pieces and placed on blueprints, it becomes difficult to have rites in which the whole community meets. The one-dimensional thinking of management tends to fulfill the functions previously discharged by collective rites, but individuals have trouble finding "private" rites which satisfy them. In a society where roles are rationally divided in this way, it is difficult to see what can bring the community together in order to celebrate its existence. In a society where people feel they only "live" in their private existences, how can we celebrate the totality of existence and the working life? How can we celebrate in a society where what is public and connected with society is of little interest compared with what is individual and private?

Destructured by industrial society, groups and communities react in various ways. Some create new types of celebrations. Thus, for the working class or for groups which reject a certain established (dis)order, demonstrations and strikes function as ritual celebrations. The upper middle classes, more affected by an isolated existence, tend to turn to psychologists and sensitivity groups of all kinds as soon as the tensions of life are too strong. They appreciate sacramental celebrations in private houses; they turn easily to celebrations of nature, based on elements which escape social conflicts, but these celebrations often assume such an individual form that they end up sounding hollow. Sometimes what comes to the fore is, above all, an absence of rite; this is especially the case at secular funerals where one is short of the traditions with which to live deeply the felt separation. This is why many people nevertheless ultimately approach the parish priest, who, whatever may sometimes be the poverty of his celebrations, is still the heir to traditions which allow him to render the celebrations not totally empty; the teaching of the church enables many, even unreligious people, to get in touch with and to tame the separation of death. Our secular society sometimes also calls on new legitimizing bodies. For example, the United Nations Organization has taken over a function from the churches in instituting years of the child, of women, of human rights; by these initiatives it has established types of "legitimizing founding accounts" by means of which contradiction-laden social relationships can be confronted. More often still, it is marketing which summons people to celebrate mothers, then fathers, then St. Valentine, etc.

But these secular attempts are to some extent revivals. In our society it is principally the one-dimensional scientific mind-set that supplies the framework for social relationships. Things happen because of technical requirements. For example, while traditional rites (carnivals, sacraments, harvest festivals) are losing ground and "going commercial," the break in daily life is marked by weekends and holidays. The rhythm of the weekend is the product of a transaction which originates in the ritual Sunday rest, which also marked a break in daily routine, but the weekend today enables the domain of private life (what belongs to oneself) to be separated completely from the domain of work. Likewise, going away on holiday is a way of proclaiming that despite everything, one has something of one's own that, at least in part, escapes imposed and programmed monotony. However, this break in time, this "transgression" in which one does what one wants, is reintegrated and taken back by society where the holidays themselves are programmed and commercialized. These developments reveal the way in which rites work in our society and how they are related to societal conflicts and tensions; they raise, among other things, the question of what Christian rites, the sacraments, have become.

Models of Christian rites and popular religions

Why do the rites of our Christian West often appear dead? By what evolution has history bequeathed us celebrations which have lost contact with daily life and its contradictions?

In the Middle Ages, the rites of the church did not yet have the rather rigid aspect which they assumed after the Reformation. While theologians noted the difference between various rites, little use was as yet made of the distinction, common today, between sacraments (first-class rites, if one may so term them, instituted by Jesus and central to the existence of the people of God) and sacramentals (second-class rites instituted by human beings and sometimes recognized by the church). While at least from the 13th century Christian communities had recognized the seven sacraments, it was only gradually that the distinction between sacraments and sacramentals became clarified. In the Middle Ages some went so far as to count 120 "sacraments" (others even listed 365, another symbolic number). Around these "sacraments" evolved a popular religion which raised the eyebrows of theologians and clerics concerned that the church should avoid superstition. They were not wrong, in fact. The part played by these abuses in triggering off the Protestant Reformation is known. Some preachers, contemporaries of Luther, even said that at the very moment a Christian gave alms the souls in purgatory were delivered! In the face of these abuses (which tend to remind us of some manifestations of devotion to St. Rita, St. Anthony and others), it is understandable that clerics wished to restore order.

Basically, the stiffness of many sacramental theologies after the Reformation is, according to some sociologists, a part of the perpetual struggle present in all cultures between learned and popular religions. People live their religion as they feel their life, both limited and aspiring to liberation. That is why the popular religions convey equally the alienations of a culture and the cries calling for liberation. In the face of certain rites one can only react because they alienate people. Witness, for example, the rite of female circumcision by which women throughout whole continents are mutilated. In the framework of Western culture it is difficult not to perceive there an oppression against which we would fight. Likewise, when thousands of people go on a pilgrimage for apparently futile reasons, this seems extremely superstitious to us "serious" people. But is this case so clear? Might there not be something else involved?

After all, what does being superstitious mean? At what moment does a rite deserve such a description? Does it not depend on your point of view? The rite which *I* live with great intensity, getting in touch with the tensions and contradictions of *my* life, might it not be seen as superstitious by another? Might not the most realistic definition of superstition be: "Superstition is other people's ritual!"? Seen from inside, rites are what all human actions are: They convey both liberation and alienation or exploitation. To them can be applied the description given by Luther to the church: "both sinful and holy." The same description, however, can be applied to the orthodoxy and the theological order which one wishes to impose on populations; do they not also sometimes convey social oppressions and alienation?

Here there is matter for reflection for specialists, theologians or others, who wish to put order into popular rites, as also for all those who think they can determine by reasoning when the sacraments lose their meaning, and for those who believe they can easily discern when it is desirable to baptize (or not to baptize) a child, or to officiate (or not to officiate) at a Christian marriage for a couple requesting it. We should send away back to back both those who allow popular piety to dictate to the people of God a false spontaneity, and those who wish to decide for it what rites are "superstitious" and to forbid them. These are two ways of not taking people seriously and of imposing an order on them which comes from outside their experience. The ossification of Christian rituals with which we are familiar today is perhaps due to this dual form of clerical religion.

At the Reformation, Luther and others (Catholics as well as Protestants) realized that the multiplicity of rituals did the people an injustice and in the end served interests other than those of the proclamation of Jesus crucified and resurrected. They led to the enslavement of the people and became, in Marx's well-chosen phrase, an effective opiate. The Protestant reaction was a radical one; it retained as sacraments only the two rites most obviously linked to Jesus by the scriptures: baptism and holy communion. The Catholic reformation kept the seven sacraments of the medieval theologians. However, the difference between the various Christian denominations on this point is perhaps less serious than appears at first sight. Furthermore, very untheological factors have doubtless played a part. The north of Europe was already more advanced than the south in the institution of a highly bourgeois mercantile society; its distrust of the rituals of the Catholic south probably match the emergence of a new rationality more interested in calculating than in celebrating. However, in both north and south, with the advance of industrialization, it became in time increasingly difficult to celebrate rites, inasmuch as these can never be completely rationalized. On the Catholic side, a sacramental theology developed which tried to say *exactly* and once and for all what is celebrated, with a resultant tendency to neglect the symbolic character of rites having multiple meanings, which, moreover, vary according to place and time.

In thus trying to construct an a-historic theology, it was overlooked that, as we have seen, symbols have their meaning only in the cultural and historical context in which they are used. This strengthened a trend to present celebrations simply as worship, separate from the concrete conflicts lived by people. This is how the Latin Mass survived until recently, even in the countries of Asia and Africa, with a priest, his back to the people, accomplishing a fixed ritual, for people who took scarcely any part. And, a typical reaction, these people were invited to do something other than what the priest was doing, for example, to pray their rosary! In one and the same celebration a learned and elitist devotion thus went together with popular piety; the two perhaps did good and harm equally at the same time.

At the time of the liturgical reform which followed Vatican Council II, the glaring liturgical errors were corrected but hardly any change was made regarding the core of the problem; there were still clerics who decided for the rest, leaving the populations hardly any opportunity to take their celebrations into their own hands. A learned theology centralized in the Vatican wanted to regulate the reform without leaving enough room for the nonrational in any ritual celebration, and without perhaps taking enough account of the place made for the people of God in the ecclesiology of Vatican II.

At the time of these recent liturgical reforms, some

Christians complained at the replacement of celebrations by discussions and reasoning. There they put their fingers on an important question: the place of reflection in celebrations. Perhaps they were not entirely wrong in complaining of an excess of intellectualism. For, while it is important during a celebration to recall and listen to the accounts concerning the founding of rites, they cannot be replaced by theology, discussions or exchanges. The distinctive nature of rational discussion is, in fact, the quest for one meaning. But, as we have seen, the rite, on the contrary, is a symbol with multiple meanings. Rite thereby seems to be a more basic way of knowing than reason, a supposition which agrees with a traditional insight that sacramental life is more important to the church than theology. The former celebrates the very life of the people of God, while the latter is always a reasoning "possessed" in varying degrees by an elite, if not by a caste of clerics. Theology is a critical authority, but it cannot claim to replace or even govern the life of Christian communities.

The stakes of ritual celebrations

Rites have concrete effects on people and groups; they convey liberations and social oppressions of various types. They do not fall from the sky; in fact, they are the expression of societal struggles. For instance, in the case of female circumcision, it is easy to see that such rituals are closely related to the social structure of man/woman relationships in the societies which practice them. It is perhaps not for us to judge, but one has to make choices; thus, I do not see how I can support such rites. Without considering such extreme cases, we have to take a stance regarding a host of "religious" or "profane" rituals which involve societal issues, such as Mother's Day, Father's Day, marriage rites, etc. Regarding this last example, one can observe how these celebrations today generally focus on the couple; there was a time—perhaps not completely gone—when marriage served primarily the interests of a social stability that benefited the established order. The vacation ritual is likewise linked to a producer and consumer society. As regard confirmation, one may wonder whether what young people commit themselves to is not sometimes the support of an establishment (an established order or disorder). On close examination, each rite and celebration shows its relationship to society. The ever-present social implications in ritual celebrations are not surprising if it is true that one of the functions of the rite is to put us in contact with the tensions and conflicts of existence. Rites are not, therefore, simply fine ceremonies of public worship or rejoicing; they are points at which human existence itself and its meanings are at stake.

It is therefore not astonishing that Christian traditions have seen in rites the place where the love of God and its struggle against evil is revealed in a very special fashion. The Christian sacraments cannot be understood if this dimension is not seen; God is revealed in them but not in simply any way. God is revealed in them in the middle of societal struggle the stake of which is human liberation. In theological terms, the Christian message does not speak of love in general but rather of redemption and salvation.

In the face of what is at stake for society in terms of its rites, we can re-examine the question of their "perversion." For instance, one can say that a rite is perverted when, instead of helping toward contact with individual and collective tensions and contradictions, it camouflages and masks them, hence serving the established authorities but not the participants. For example, an organized mass demonstration, such as sometimes takes place in Moscow or Peking, appears to me to be a perversion of the very thing it purports to be. While demonstrations can help in perceiving and living the contradictions in society, they have an opposite effect when they are organized by the authorities themselves to hide these contradictions. On the contrary, when a rite is true, it tends to be subversive since it brings out tensions and contradictions which would not have been perceived otherwise.

Understanding of salvation and Christian liberation produces criteria which make it possible to state what is understood here by the "perversion" of a sacrament. A sacrament is "perverted" if, instead of being a rite of liberation, it serves the mystery of evil (symbolized in theology by the concept of original sin and in social analysis by concepts of oppression and exploitation). Thus, the Eucharist is "subversive" and serves liberation when it clearly reveals the death of Jesus as that of a torture victim who trusted in his Father to the end. But when it is reduced to a pleasant celebration in which all is harmony, it is distortion since such reduction masks the conflicts inherent in all human decisions. We shall have to examine each of the sacraments in order to discover its liberating and its perverted forms. It will be necessary to do this without introducing a new theology which would again make decisions in place of the people.

These considerations make it possible to shed light on a frequent debate among Christians: When should rites be considered pagan? Such problems have always been encountered; for example, in the 18th century at the time of the "Chinese rite" dispute. In that case, Western Christians did not accept Chinese rituals, on the grounds that they were superstitious and pagan.[2] But at least some Christian rites have roots in pagan celebrations, so this cannot be a sufficient reason for rejecting them.

Would it not be better to ask oneself which are the rites that liberate individuals and groups, and which are those that oppress them? For the former are compatible with the founding account of Jesus' death and resurrection, while the latter are not. As St. Paul says, liberation in Jesus Christ reaches all that is human, without distinction as to pagan or Jew, pagan or Christian.

In any case, one must refrain from describing rites as pagan simply because they are not controlled by theology. Very often, in fact, people wish to celebrate significant moments in their existence and to give them a religious expression, without necessarily being interested in theological argument. For example, I remember the funeral of an old man in a very poor neighborhood. Since he had been on welfare and without any family, no

---

2. This refusal damaged Christianity in China. It was only recently that Rome, through the pronouncements of Pius XI, officially modified its attitude on this point.

ceremony had been arranged. When he was ready to be taken away, there were only a few of us in front of the coffin made of several planks. It could be felt in a confused way that these people, far removed as they were from the church's institutions, wanted to do something to "mark the occasion." We then celebrated this separation by a prayer, the content of which was ultimately of little importance. Afterwards, those present said with a kind of relief, "He wasn't buried like a dog." Superstition, some will say! I do not think so; rather it shows a desire on the part of those people to live in a human way, despite the second-class status they had been given by society. Who am I, a priest set apart by my training, to pass the slightest judgment on that life experience? What I am certain of is that this celebration was good for them; I cannot say the same for all the sacraments, even when carried out according to all the rules. The question as to what exactly is lived by the people who celebrate a rite is quite as inadequate as that of a lover who asks his or her partner exactly what the other feels. This type of question reduces a much richer experience to the one dimension of an intellectual argument. On the other hand, questions which concern the effects of ritual celebrations are very relevant: What have these celebrations accomplished for the persons and groups concerned? Are their effects liberating or are they oppressive? Do they express the hope and liberation of the poor, or are they the instruments of control by those who happen to be the governing classes of the moment? Have they enabled people to discover the profoundest dimensions of their existence, including the ultimate call of a transcendental dimension?

Leaders of rites and their regulation

To live out celebrations, leaders of rites are needed, or "ministers of worship," to use a different type of language. They are necessary for any community celebration, since without them the ceremonies are liable to become the exclusive possession of "the big mouth." However, the role of such ministers is ambiguous. Some leaders use their role to bring communities back into the established order which they represent. As if they possessed a monopoly of the Holy Spirit, they deprive populations of their history; they make them enter a life programmed by the reasoning of the experts—or, worse still, by their own views—in accordance with the established order (disorder). Other leaders, however, have the charisma to lead a community through rites in such a way that it can take over its own life and history, express its conflicts symbolically, and begin to resolve them in the hope of a more thorough liberation, in behalf of which it acts and wages its struggle.

It is probably necessary to reassess this role of rite leader, which has too often fallen into discredit as a result of the ossification of the sacraments. Priests are sometimes heard complaining that they are there just to administer sacraments in the manner of magicians. Yet, from the viewpoint we have outlined, the question presents itself quite differently! To help a community to celebrate in suitable rites is an important ministry . . . at least if one knows how to do it. Leading a rite is a social role at least as important as that of a psychologist or manager; it is helping a group to get in touch with what is deepest in it, its hopes, its struggles, its contradictions, its joys and pains, the manifestations of the transcendental. It is not a question of programming celebrations for the masses but of working with them to enable them to discern liberating rites and to free themselves from celebrations which alienate or serve oppressive structures. Helping a community to welcome a new member, to listen seriously to his or her voice as coming from God, to celebrate forgiveness, to live in trust decisions leading to the unknown, to approach death alone but not lonely, to hope in the very human institution of marriage and the family, to find the manifestation of God in the tensions entailed by all human power, all this is by no means negligible! It is a collective and individual service that is perhaps more important than many other "ministries" fulfilled by the clergy.

In every community, rite leaders have a real power; the way in which they promote or check contact with what is lived by the group in depth, with its conflicts and contradictions, will ultimately influence the group's development. They can encourage rites, whether perverted or subversive. In any event, rites will partly determine the unity of the group in one way or another. It is therefore not astonishing that communities should introduce some regulation of rites, such that individuals cannot direct them completely as they wish. In the church, such regulation is effected by the bishops—the monitors—assisted by the critical reflection of the theologians, itself inspired by the life of communities. The task of the bishops is to see that Christian rites are not diverted from their function: to reveal God as the liberator from all forms of oppression. It is important that the church should not let itself be co-opted to the point of allowing the perversion of its rites, which would then serve domination by the "powers of this world."

What is observed in the church also occurs in all societies: Rituals contribute to social integration, give structure to communities, and enable societal tensions to be lived with. However, they can do so in various ways, and with different purposes; that is why they are the expression of sociopolitical conflicts. As factors of social integration, rites put social relationships on an institutional footing; whether around a salute to the flag or a Eucharist, they build communities. An important thing is to see which groups in society are being supported.

2 | Christian Sacraments and Society's Conflicts

In strict logic a survey of the "sacraments in general" should follow rather than precede examination of the various sacramental practices. The latter in fact come first, theory only systematizing what is first lived. In the case of rites, even more so than for other social actions, practice is first and is in no way deduced from theory. To make the survey simple, however, it may be useful to present a general theory first, provided the pedagogic nature of this procedure is seen. Sacramental theology is reflection on the practices of Jesus and of Christian communities; these are the historical events of salvation and cannot be deduced from a theory. They express the gift of God.

The central current of Christian tradition asserts that the sacraments are rites of the church, instituted by Jesus Christ, efficacious in themselves and producing the gracious gift of God which they signify. Such a definition calls for a comment, for it can be understood to mean many things.

First of all, sacraments are rites. Rites are not magic gestures. They are a living expression of the participants, who act out and express a profound reality which they endeavor to explore. Rites do not function on the level of univocal language but on that of symbols; the explanation that is given of them can never claim to exhaust their meaning. They refer to a whole societal context outside which they appear, quite simply, alien. As they have multiple meanings, they are particularly vulnerable to social manipulation. Very little is needed for them to be perverted, turned aside from their original aim, and made to serve special interests. Furthermore, insofar as they establish contact with profound contradictions in society, they have a subversive aspect. In any case, they are not neutral.

Rites of the church

The sacraments are rites of the church. This statement calls for a number of comments. First of all, they are not individual rites. In all cultures, rites exist which affect individuals and their relationships. The sacraments affect the community of Christians; it is the community as a group which lives the sacraments, well beyond what is lived by each participant and by the leaders of rites. Analyses of sacraments which speak only of what happens to a person are therefore too limited. For example, the sacrament of the sick does not concern solely an individual whose life is threatened but the whole community which lives with him or her. The same applies to all the sacraments. It is particularly important to stress this point in a society which tends to isolate individuals.

The sacraments are also rites of the church in the sense that it is the church community that summons its members to celebrate and to confront tensions and contradictions which they might otherwise forget or cover up. This is also true for other challenges by the church (which are not called "sacraments") such as the seasons of Lent and Advent and funeral services. In inviting people to celebrate these feasts, the church prompts communities and individuals to go beyond the superficial aspects of life and to face realities which are too easily concealed. For instance, in the Eucharist, the memorial of Jesus' giving up his life in the conflict which brought him into opposition with the high priests continues to confront Christians with the questions: Why did Jesus die? Why was he put with thieves? Why do we die? Why do we struggle? In the celebration of baptism, the traditions that speak of original sin have sometimes forced certain communities to face the fact that the world and society are not all harmonious and problem free. The entrance of a new member, especially if it is a child, refers the community to sometimes haunting questions: Will the child find a community which will love it unconditionally or will that child be crushed by human oppression? What sort of community are we and will we be to him or her? These questions do not refer to morality but confront society with its contradictions.

This confrontation with challenging traditions also provides a key with which to analyze rites and a method for those who seek ways to celebrate. One can indeed always assume that tradition leads somewhere and that it speaks of society's contradictions and tensions experienced by those who instituted it. It can similarly be assumed that rites which no longer reveal an important dimension of existence must have been diverted on the way. Thus, when we hear baptism spoken of as if it were a somewhat magical gesture to expunge a stain from the child's soul, we may wonder what kind of ideological manipulation succeeded in imposing an interpretation which to us appears somewhat ridiculous. What reality was so threatening and so subversive that it became necessary to render it insipid and ridiculous? In the case of baptism and the other sacraments we shall see that ideological mechanisms tend to make a tradition meaningless precisely when it has something important to disclose. To understand the misadventures of the sacraments and of their interpretations one has to relate them to the concrete history of communities and societies.

The rites founding the church community

The sacraments are of the church, for it is the church that invites people to celebrate them. It can also be said that, ultimately, they constitute the church; there is no distinction to be made between the church community and the community that lives the sacramental rites. Christians often wonder what community is the church. Some see it as the hierarchy, others look to the faithful as a whole; but what comes probably closest to Christian traditions—and to anthropological sensitivity—is to say that the church is the community which celebrates sacraments. Such a point of view allies theological traditions with the sociological intuition of Durkheim, for whom religious celebrations give structure to communities. Placing the foundation of the church in the sacraments has another advantage: It links the church to events of a symbolic nature and thus avoids the one-dimensionality involved in any other type of logic, be it hierarchical or theological. Asserting that the church is the community celebrating the gift of God in the sacraments places it in the middle of the tensions and conflicts which traverse human societies, without in any way identifying it with a particular policy or ideology (although political and ideological tensions are conveyed by the church's celebrations). When the Christian assembly (the church) appears as a sacrament (a ritual celebration with all that it implies, among other things contact with society's contradictions), it can reveal salvation and redemption by showing that the gracious gift of God (grace) is manifested in the midst of a world full of contradictions (i.e., "marked by original sin"). When, on the other hand, the church appears simply in the form of a hierarchy and orthodoxy, it veils the reality of salvation in apparent but spurious clarity. Saying that the church is a sacrament therefore not only agrees with a profound traditional intuition but also situates hierarchy and orthodoxy in their place at the service of the sacraments.

Rites instituted by Jesus Christ

The institution of the sacraments by Jesus Christ has assumed a fairly important place in theological treatises, especially since the Reformation. As the Protestants kept two sacraments and the Catholics seven, the question arose as to why. The Protestants justified their clean sweep of all the sacraments or sacramentals of the Middle Ages by pointing out that scripture contained clear statements concerning the institution of the Eucharist and baptism only. Catholics, for their part, laid stress on the institution of the seven sacraments by Christ. One could therefore expect to see theological considerations put forward regarding the role of Jesus instituting—and therefore legitimizing—the sacraments.

In fact, theologians stressed the institution of the sacraments but this did not always facilitate understanding of the sacramental rites. In many Catholic theologies, the concept of institution of the sacraments became formalist: The sacrament was important because Jesus had said, "Do this," and not because *in* this ritual celebration the community can encounter the gift of God, in the middle of its tensions. For example, many Catholics interpreted the command, "Do this in memory of me" of the Last Supper in a highly minimalist way, by suggesting that Jesus gave authority to certain ministers of worship to carry out ritual gestures only; they did not perceive that Jesus was thereby inviting his disciples to give and share their lives, as he was doing himself. Theological systems were built in which rites found their value not in celebration but, by an external effect, in a grace which was ultimately *added* to the sacrament. Such a theological process tends to interpret the sacrament in a magical way, if this is taken to mean an approach aimed at obtaining in a manner external to the community a power over what happens in the community. This belief in external intervention (and not in intervention inherent in the sacrament) in the long run encouraged sacramental celebrations in which people no longer participated and no longer celebrated anything; they were there simply to receive "the grace of the sacrament" without the rite impinging on their existence, psychology and social relations. From this stemmed the habit, itself recommended at the time by the hierarchy, of saying the rosary during the Eucharist.

Fortunately, the situation is different nowadays, and for the past 30 years theologians have restored the importance of the liturgies themselves (although in the clerical religion with which we are familiar conducting the liturgy is often still considered by many priests and Christians to be a less important, less "serious" or less humanly fulfilling ministry than that of the theologians, or that of guidance, preaching or social work!). But there was still the problem of Jesus' institution of the sacraments. The question became increasingly awkward, for the progress of exegesis and the history of the primitive church made the evidence convincing: The Protestants had not been wrong to point out that it was difficult to derive certain rites from scripture, and even from the most ancient traditions. The idea of foundation was expanded—actually rediscovering some ancient theological traditions: Jesus had instituted the essence of the sacraments, but the forms of the celebrations were fixed by the church. This idea was shrewd but it smacked strangely of unreality compared with what is felt by a community which lives and celebrates.

In order to clarify the question it was undoubtedly necessary to re-center it. This has been done by a number of theologians over the past 50 years by stressing the fact that the only sacrament was, in its own way, the person of Jesus himself. It is he who, in the activities of his life, in his death and resurrection, effects the transition Passover, which is the founding event of Christianity and ultimately the only Christian rite. In the end, in another sense, it is the church, the community of the people of God assembled by Jesus and living in his Spirit, which is the place of salvation, the only sacrament of Christians.

In this way, the question of the origin of the sacraments can be resituated in the totality of the life of Christian communities; the institution of the sacraments by Jesus can be attributed to the risen Christ living in the church and in each and every Christian. From this point of view it becomes possible to see the direct action of Christ and his Spirit in the various communal mechanisms which structure sacramental rites and which, moreover, continue to modify them. With this viewpoint it is no longer necessary to return to a reconstructed past in order to give legitimacy to what is lived today. The new must no longer be sought in the past (sometimes treating very lightly the criteria of historical research). The church is then perceived as a living community which, by the Spirit who lives in it, creates its own symbols and which reinterprets rites of the past (without necessarily asking itself whether they are Christian or pagan). Faith in the presence of Jesus risen and active among his people can thus save sacramental practices from the straitjacket of rationalist theologies which stifle them. However, it is still important to spell out the relationships of the sacraments with the founding event: the life of Jesus (in theological terms, the incarnation).

Rites instituted by the liberating practices of Jesus

There is, I believe, an important message in the Christian traditions which remind us that "the sacraments were instituted by Jesus." I should therefore like to re-read these traditions, reflecting on what the confrontation with Jesus "instituting" the sacraments may actually mean to a community.

Every rite, as we have seen, refers in one way or another to founding accounts. These accounts can doubtless be re-read, reinterpreted and subjected to "transactions," but they are resistant in the sense that they cannot be made to mean just anything. Thus, I find it difficult to liken Jesus to someone who supports the powerful of this world, those who are "dressed in silks and satins" and live in "palaces" (Mt 11:8). The Bible resists such readings in that they appear to many Christians to be incompatible with an obvious interpretation of scripture. That, in my view, is the deepest intuition contained in the traditions which attribute the sacraments to Jesus: One does not so much say that Jesus left a particular instruction as that, by his practice and the reading he makes of his actions, Jesus gives a meaning to certain rites.

I believe, therefore, that when we say that Jesus instituted the Eucharist the most important assertion is the reference to the practice of Jesus, living to the very end—that is, in the face of his death as a criminal—the conflicts and struggles in which he was engaged, while placing his trust in the Father. When we say that Jesus instituted the sacrament of forgiveness, strictly speaking I am not much interested in knowing whether there was a moment when Jesus said this rite must be practiced; what interests me much more is the practice of forgiveness which Jesus instituted in his very living and which the Christian community wishes to continue in the sacrament of forgiveness. In this sense, to celebrate the sacrament is to live forgiveness in memory of Jesus (with all the force of what a "memorial" is in Hebrew ritual tradition); it is to discover that in communal forgiveness the total forgiveness of the Father is also revealed. We could continue in this way for all the sacraments; they do not seem to me to have been instituted so much by a *command* of Jesus as by his *practice*. The most important point is that Jesus instituted practices which are celebrated in Christian rites; in this sense, I have no doubt that Jesus instituted the sacraments.

Furthermore, since the liberating practices of Jesus in his society institute the rites performed in memory of him, they continue to be the criteria for the Christian authenticity of the sacramental rites. The central criterion of the Christian authenticity of a sacrament does not therefore lie primarily in rules defined by theology; the main point is whether this celebration in fact produces the fruits of the kingdom of Jesus in accordance with his liberating practices. In this sense, to be Christian, the sacraments must celebrate the confrontation of Jesus with the mystery of evil in the world; that is, in St. Thomas' expression, celebrate the passion of Christ. And it is not only the passion of the historical Christ but also that of Christ living in his people today. Christian communities will always have to be converted in order to ensure that it is really the liberation in Christ, the salvation of Christ, that is celebrated in their assemblies. All Christians are responsible but special responsibility is borne by the leaders of rites (ministers of the sacraments) and by the bishops.

From this viewpoint, we can speak of the institution of the sacraments by Jesus without worrying whether he had any particular type of rite in mind. Such a viewpoint frees us from the cultural constraints of an epoch or a nation. One may ask oneself, for example, with Tissa Balasuriya, the Sri Lankan theologian, what the point was of importing Western wine for the celebration of the Eucharist in countries which did not know this drink. Does not this resemble the rejection of the "Chinese rites" to which I have alluded above? Was not the liberating institution of Jesus being perverted by submitting countries unjustly colonized by the West to Western cultural features? Attributing such importance to these material factors is doubtless a kind of materialism, but this is not the most serious consideration. It seems to me that what is most serious is that this materialism actually conveys—in the guise of religion—relationships of oppression; it was also against oppression that, *in his "instituting" practices* Jesus rebelled, to the point where he was eventually put to death.

However, one should not be so keen on acculturating Christian rites as to forget that they always refer to an "elsewhere": the life and practices of Jesus (the incarnation). The Eucharist, for example, does not consist in the sharing of bread and wine as consumer goods but refers to Jesus' passion. This is also absolutely clear in traditional theologies, which speak of the sharing of his body and blood.

Again, theological traditions of the institution of the sacraments by Jesus bring out the difference between very worthy rites (such as sharing bread together) and the sacraments. The latter are not feasts which communities decide to celebrate as of that moment; they are performed explicitly in remembrance of Jesus and they fit into a Christian "history of salvation." In this reading of history, communities abandon the usual historical accounts (always written by the conquerors); they see the hope coming from God in a crucified outcast (unimportant as far as official Roman history is concerned), in a man who proclaims and lives without measure, forgiveness and the gratuitous gift of God. Christian sacraments are linked to this reading of our present history through the history of salvation; they lead to the discovery of the latter, over and above other readings. They make it possible to live the sacred, i.e. the most profound dimension of things, as the place where the liberation coming from God to Jesus becomes manifest and real in our societies.

When one thinks it over, the foregoing considerations are a paraphrase of what St. Thomas asserted when he said that the sacraments (in particular, the Eucharist) celebrate the grace of God (gratuitous love), the passion of

Christ (the confrontation with evil in the world) and the glory to come (hope of total liberation in the kingdom).

Efficacious signs

While, in popular piety, the efficacy of the sacraments has often taken on a magical appearance, theological traditions are generally more reserved. I consider it pointless to go into the details of the systems devised in order to explain that it is the action of the church (of the Christian community) and not of any particular one of its members (ministers of the sacraments) which is important for the efficacy of the rite. To me it seems more important to come back to the efficacy specific to ritual celebrations.

When celebrated by a community which lives them, rites transform that community. This is as true of a properly performed Eucharist as of the Nazi mass demonstrations at Nuremberg before the war. By participation in ritual celebrations, social relationships are modified and represented differently, while other ways of living them are accepted. These transformations affect collective representations as well as individual psychologies. Is it not strange that certain sacramental theologies which nevertheless wished to present the incarnation as the center of their reflection have almost produced opposite effects?

However, according to Christian traditions, there is more in the sacraments than efficacious rites, by virtue of the sociopsychological mechanisms which they set in motion; Christians believe that the mystery of the freeing action of *God* is at work. The efficacy of sacramental rites, when they are not perverted, refers to this long coming of God's liberating power in the course of history. All Christian rites refer to the redemption, i.e., to the confrontation between the liberating love of God and the mystery of evil. Christian faith therefore affirms that God's power is at work in the face of the tensions of existence. The sacraments thus refer to these tensions, more specifically to those which are linked to the coming of a new member, to the acquisition of a voice in matters, to the wounds inflicted by one person upon another, to decisions taken, to confrontation with death, to the institution of marriage or of power in a community; it is in these tensions that the liberating God is revealed. The purpose of the celebrations is to bring communities to recognize a manifestation of God in these various circumstances.

The sacraments do not therefore have the aim of causing people to be good; contrary to what even most current practice might suggest, they are not moralizing. To persons about to be confirmed, the point is not to say, as is sometimes said, that henceforward they must take care that what is expressed in them is truly the Spirit. On the contrary, confirmation must by its liturgical *action,* by its rite, bring the confirmees and their community to face the fact that *the Spirit is in them.* The sacraments are not rule-giving programs of action but, instead, events involving a meeting with God present in our societies. In traditional terms, the non-moralizing character of the sacraments used to be expressed by saying that they conferred grace, that is, the gratuitous gift of God. They act as a "feast" acts, by making it possible to live things in depth, to "mark the occasion." The sacraments are Christian only if, like Jesus, they cease to be moralizing in order to reveal the gracious gift of God.

Linked to the non-moralizing character of the sacraments is the assertion that it is not the individual who acts in the sacrament but God through the church (the Christian community). An individual is not asked initially to act in a particular way in order to be fit to receive the sacrament, but initially it is the church that is called upon to make the liberating action of God manifest to individuals and groups. From this point of view, at a baptism, for example, the question changes from the usual: "Has the new member faith?" to another question addressed to the community: "How are we going to live in order that the new member may discover the love of God and therefore have faith?" The first viewpoint sets a moral for an individual, while the second leads the group to discover the call and the gift of God within it. Such viewpoints are to be underlined in order that sacramental celebrations may lose the characteristic they sometimes have of making people feel guilty or even of crushing them.

But have we not simply shifted the emphasis of the question? Even if the individual is not made to feel guilty, the problem remains: Is not the community, being always imperfect, liable to find its celebrations empty and unproductive? How, for example, can a sinful community full of contradictions manifest God's love to a child? (It should be added that, seeing the church as it is, young couples sometimes decide not to have their children baptized.) How can we speak of the sacraments' efficacy when it is clear that they are celebrating a liberation which is still only in its beginning stages? In fact, celebrations are performed against the background of an ideal which they never fully achieve. In theological language, we say that the sacraments speak of an eschatological reality; St. Thomas said that the sacraments speak of "the glory of God," of the glory to come. Rites act by evoking a reality which has not yet been achieved. Thus, a birthday supper, like the sacraments, evokes an image of mutual relations which does not correspond to the reality of everyday routine; but it is by living the ideal symbolically in a celebration that new social links are also fashioned and that the contradictions of the daily round are brought face to face with the ideal. As a result, something happens. The same goes for the sacraments. It is quite clear that no Christian community is so transparent to God's love that it can reveal it unambiguously, to the point of giving faith. Nevertheless, despite all the ambiguities, it is this utopian reality which is sought and it is through the *symbolic* and *ritual* acting out of a true community of love that baptism "gives faith." It often happens at a good baptismal celebration, moreover, that after the "feast" participants feel linked to the new Christian in a new and different way; the rite has produced its effect by creating a new relationship which changes existence and enlivens the church, i.e., the community of salvation.

Are the sacraments necessary?   When are they valid?

The question of the efficacy of the sacraments introduces another traditional question: Does one need the sacraments? Too often this question is considered in the context of a "need of God," whereas the reply becomes simple if it is situated on the level of human psychology. We need the sacraments because we cannot live alone; for our life to have meaning, it is important to "mark the occasion" together, to get in touch with the tensions of existence, and to evoke in some celebration the hope on which we live. The realities symbolized in a sacrament will live in us only if we celebrate them sometimes, in one way or another. The sacraments are therefore necessary, not so much as a condition required by God for "salvation" but because one can live in depth only if one celebrates what one lives.

The efficacy of the sacraments has often been linked to their validity. Unfortunately this question has often obscured the very meaning of the celebrations; attempts were made to find out whether the celebration was "valid" and not to see whether it was consistent with the passion of Christ and whether it produced the effects of the kingdom. Validity is a legal concept which corresponds to a very simple question: What are the celebrations which the church recognizes as its own because they agree with the practices of Jesus? Those celebrations will be called "valid." Put thus, the question of the validity of the sacraments arises only if certain parties dispute the recognition of the celebration by the church. If a group of Christians celebrates the mystery of the life, death and resurrection of Jesus as it is lived in that group, the important thing for the group is that it celebrates, and not the abstract concept of "validity." The sacraments are real when they truly produce their effect, namely, the manifestation of the liberating power of God in Jesus, the confrontation of love and evil, the hope of the kingdom. These effects are the first evidences of the value of the rites; as the Bible says, it is the fruits of the kingdom that must be considered: If they are present, it has to be recognized that the tree is sound. One should listen to the recommendation of Jesus, made before those very people who did not dare to read the "signs of the times": "And why can you not judge for yourselves what is the right thing to do?" (Lk 12:57). This being said, it is understandable that the church should indicate the rules which it considers should be complied with in the celebrations, in order to give them official recognition. And these rules are useful for understanding the way in which the church calls us to celebrate in memory of Jesus. One would have to be naive, however, to believe that the grace of God, God's gracious love, reveals itself only through these rules; just as it would be naive to believe that it is revealed automatically as soon as those rules are respected.

Conclusions

The foregoing considerations make it possible to propose certain criteria for assessing sacramental celebrations. First of all, when a sacrament is perceived as an individual event, something is not quite right, as it is the Christian community, the church, which acts in the sacrament. What is transformed by the ritual celebration is not simply an individual but a community, and through it a society. Again, the sacraments cannot be moralizing; they speak of the gratuitous or gracious gift of God and not of what must be done. Neither do they speak of just any God but of the Father of Jesus and of Jesus himself. And Jesus is the one who was tortured to death in the middle of the thieves because he had chosen his loyalties toward the poor, the little ones and the oppressed. The sacraments which do not reveal that the good news is addressed to the poor are not the sacraments instituted by the practices of Jesus Christ. And as the sacraments cause Christians to relive what Jesus lived, they will, like the practices of Jesus themselves, be considered subversive according to the criteria of the established order. Furthermore, sacramental celebrations celebrate the confrontation between the love of God and the mystery of evil; consequently they must evoke tensions and conflicts, both individual and collective. Finally, the sacraments as rites do not concern ideas alone but the body and even the social body, with all the structures linked thereto. The sacraments are intended to reveal the liberations which come from God; and yet it must be expected that they are often diverted and used by the ideologies of the moment; the kingdom of God, although already present, remains a promise recalled by the celebrations but not yet fulfilled. They are also a hope that can be lived in the joy and tenderness of a community which discovers itself loved therein.

3 | Eucharist: Celebrating the Decisions Involving Life and Death

To understand eucharistic celebrations, it is necessary to start from lived experiences. I am thinking of a Eucharist celebrated by striking workers in the waiting room of a law court, of another taking place in a hospital room on the eve of a dangerous operation, or another celebrated by a community of nuns who, the same morning, had resigned en masse from a hospital where they had been working for years but whose social policy they no longer accepted. I am thinking of all the times when Christians, realizing that they were making decisions important for them or for their communities, remembered Jesus who, on the eve of his death, shared his life with his friends. That evening Jesus made a decision from which there was no turning back, and accepted living to the end the consequences of his loyalties. In eucharistic celebrations, Christians commemorate this passage lived by Jesus; they do this at the moment when they too find themselves facing decisions from which there is no return, and important choices in matters of responsibility. To live the Eucharist is to live the decisions and risks taken in living, in conjunction with Jesus' decision to give his life.

The founding accounts of the Eucharist

The founding account of the eucharistic rite is that of Jesus' commitment to a radicalism which ultimately cost him his life. The Last Supper is no longer the moment of discussion or of the actual struggle; Jesus has already lived these and the Pharisees have learned to recognize in him an adversary of stature whom it is impossible to dismiss easily. The Last Supper is not even the moment for the important choices of his life. He had already made these choices long before; for example, at Capernaum one Sabbath when he got angry at the Pharisees' hardness of heart and cured the man with the withered hand; it was then, moreover, as St. Mark tells us (Mk 3:6), that the Pharisees met the followers of Herod to examine how they might eliminate him. Likewise, it was not on the day when they resigned from the hospital that the nuns spoken of earlier made the most important choice; that day they only acknowledged together the choices in regard to a solidarity which had previously been made, little by little, in apparently insignificant moments. Similarly, it was not during the days preceding his assassination that Archbishop Oscar Romero made the decisions which were important to his life, but rather when he felt himself increasingly on the side of the exploited of El Salvador, to the point where he moved away from his original social background. On the evening of the Last Supper, Jesus makes his choices manifest; scarcely any other way is now open to him than to go forward and drink the cup offered to him.

To understand what is celebrated in the Eucharist, it is necessary to realize how Jesus reached that point. He had trust in him whom he calls his Father. The Bible relates it to us in the symbolic account of the baptism in the Jordan; he hears a voice saying that he is the beloved Son. He has trust and he dares to speak and act with authority. He makes choices symbolized in the account of the temptations in the desert; he does not wish to enclose people in the straitjackets of wonder-working, or the quest for bread, or of power. He wants them free. He chases away demons, he teaches in a different way from the scribes and Pharisees; the people are astonished at this new teaching which is given with authority. He goes beyond the categories of the pure and the impure by healing the leper. He is not afraid to forgive the sins of the man sick with palsy, thus showing human beings that the power of forgiveness is in their hands. He eats with sinners, takes liberties with the laws on fasting. He declares that the law was made for human beings and not human beings for the law. Stepping outside the straitjacket of the family, he refuses to be a prisoner of his clan, establishing among those who seek the liberation which comes from God a new solidarity going beyond family. This brings him into conflict with those who have other loyalties, who wish to maintain the religious and political orders necessary in order to reach an accommodation with the Roman colonial power. By his practice, Jesus puts people on their feet (he raises them up); this does not please everyone. He does not wish to silence the crowd on Palm Sunday, because once the people speak they must not be stopped; the very stones would cry out on that day, so much do people feel the liberating power of God. This goes further; arriving at the temple, he expels the merchants. It is too much; the princes of the church are jealous and, worse still, afraid. This man, who could have been one of them—for he speaks well and dominates situations—chooses solidarity with the humble and the oppressed. He is subversive. And the Romans are beginning to get anxious. These thoughts were doubtless stirring in Jesus' head on the evening he celebrated the Passover.

Passover! It speaks of the passing of God. The people were oppressed in Egypt. They were exploited, and measures were taken to ensure that they did not have too many children, such fear did they inspire. But Yahweh heard his people's cries; he ordered Moses to lead them out of Egypt. On the evening of the Passover, this liberating passing of God whereby the Jewish people had been delivered was recalled. It was not just an internal and purely spiritual liberation which would have left social exploitations as they were; it was an overall liberation which had since become the symbol of that liberation ever-present in the hope of Israel. Jesus recalled it on the evening of the Last Supper; that is what church traditions call on us to reflect upon in celebrating Eucharist.

That evening Jesus remembered the love of his Father, the trust which enabled him to speak with authority; he saw the conflicts into which his loyalties had little by little drawn him. But, even so, he could not have refrained from healing on the Sabbath day! Any more than one would leave an ox in a well on that day! This resonated in him and reminded him of the passing of Yahweh, the flight from Egypt, the Red Sea, the desert, the column of fire, and at the same time of the impossibility of finding a solution today. Cornered like many others before and after him, knowing that he could have been on the other side among the strong and the powerful, knowing that he could probably still do so or fight with the sword, he took bread, broke it and shared it with his friends saying to them, "Here is my life for you. Whenever you, too, in one way or another, are at the same point as I am now, remember me and do as I have done."

That is the story which brings Christians to meet together in the face of their decisions, their choices, the risks of their existence, in order to remember Jesus. They share their life and his life, in the form of bread, continuing thus in their lives today what he lived: his death and the sacrifice of his life in accord with his loyalties. The reality of what is acted out in the celebration is the "Here is our life" of all the members of the celebrating community, and by commemorating the gift of Jesus everyone can better understand the meaning of his or her own loyalties. In this context, there is meaning in talking of the real presence of Jesus in this sacrament.

Thus, Jesus, and Christians following his path, write a history other than that of the Roman Empire and the powerful of this world, a history other than the one which will be written by conquerors. The history of salvation (liberation) links the actions of the exploited, women, slaves, people like Jesus, of all those who have no history according to the world's usual standards. The accounts of kings and the powerful of this world make everything part of their order; by the writing of history they impose even on the past. The eucharistic celebration does not work like that. It recalls all the passings of God in history, the memory of the life, conflicts and struggles of all those who, in the footsteps of Jesus, in counterpoint to the history of the powerful, have said again and again, trusting in the Father, "Here is my life for you." That is why it is important that Christian communities "mark the occasion" by eucharistic celebrations whenever being faithful to the loyalties contracted in the footsteps of Jesus causes them to cross new frontiers, to embark on the unknown, like Jesus on the eve of the Last Supper, even to death. The persistence of these commitments "in memory of him" is the basis for the hope of Christians.

Up to now I have taken from the "founding account" all that happened before the Last Supper. But Christian traditions go further; they also include everything that Jesus experienced afterwards in his passion. Through the passion and death of Jesus people can understand the gift he made of his life, his sacrifice.

The death of Jesus and our era

In the 1960s and early 1970s, Christians and most people talked little about the death of Jesus. Death was at that time erased from most human stories, being relegated to hospital rooms where people lived out their last moments alone, surrounded by machines which kept them artificially alive. At that time most Christians preferred to speak of the resurrection. This insistence on life and this tendency to erase the death of Jesus were doubtless not alien to a mentality which trusted to progress to solve humanity's problems: Science, technology, education, and international solidarity would eliminate hunger from the world and permit the development of all countries. The majority of people had an optimistic view of history, conforming to the way in which it is written by the powerful; accordingly, the death of that outsider, Jesus, was no longer interesting. The Christs of the Byzantine Empire, glorious and triumphant like emperors, were preferred to him. But today, poverty is still with us and seems nowhere near receding; the structures of individual and collective exploitation appear stronger than ever. This causes Christians to ask themselves afresh about the death of Jesus and what they celebrate in the Eucharist. This questioning is arising nearly everywhere in the world, but particularly in Latin America, where the theologians of liberation are raising the question with new acuteness and where militants risk their lives for the liberation of human beings.

Why did Jesus die?

Since the founding of Christianity, Christians have been discomfitted by the death of Jesus and particularly by his execution, which they tend to hide; it was a scandal, absurd. And so it is if we see it with the eyes of secular history. Thus, quite quickly the title of Jesus as the "suffering servant of Yahweh" was blurred in favor of other names which put one more in mind of the resurrection, such as Messiah, Lord, Son of God, Logos. The cross moved into the background and was sometimes considered as a simple preliminary step to the resurrection. Very quickly, too, the conflict in which Jesus gave his life (in which he sacrificed himself) was muted in favor of worship of the type inveighed against by many prophets who said that sacrifices pleasing to God consisted of works of liberation. The tendency to play down the cross led to its being given a set of logical explanations which no longer had much to do with the concrete history of Jesus. Thus, the scandalous aspect of the torture of Jesus often gave way to theories explaining abstractly why it had to be so. Both yesterday and today, abstract explanations often have the result of masking the concrete conflicts of existence and society.

A fairly common way of avoiding a confrontation both with the death of Jesus and with the conflicts of society is to say that they obey a logic of necessity: It could not have been otherwise. This statement has its share of truth; Jesus (or Martin Luther King, or Romero, or Gandhi) lived in such a way that it was possible to say afterwards: "It was inevitable, society being what it is, they were bound to get themselves eliminated one day." This necessity is concrete and in no way veils society's tensions. More frequently, however, theologians have explained abstractly, sometimes almost metaphysically, why it was "bound" to be so. Some of these explanations are quite simply repugnant (yet all their effects have not yet entirely disappeared); for example, those explanations which portray the Father of Jesus, God, as a rather sadistic being who rejoices at the sufferings of his son and who agrees to forget (can we speak of forgiveness?) the sins of men because his Son was sacrificed. Other theories are saner, although they often end up being governed by the logic of power: "Is it not better that one should die for the whole people?" Traditional ideas of sacrifice thus sometimes serve to reduce the death of Jesus, and then the Eucharist, to a sort of settlement of accounts between God and people.

Other approaches seem to me to be more suitable when they stress the fact that God so loved us as to be prepared to die. "Greater love hath no man than that he should lay down his life for his friend" (Jn 15:13). These theologies link the death of Jesus to an unconditional love. I find this just, but still incomplete. These theologies tell us that God loves us but they refrain from considering the way in which God appeared as the loving one and as savior. This trend shows itself in a subtle way of eliminating the execution on the cross in the interests of more acceptable expressions such as "Jesus' death, his return to the Father," etc. These expressions do not say that he was rejected by his people, as an agitator and a marginal person, and that he was eventually executed amid thieves. In a pinch, many God-fearing people would be more comfortable with the assassination of Archbishop Romero than with the execution of Jesus; Romero at least did not die between two thieves but in a church. And, practically everywhere throughout the world, many people at once saw him as a martyr; it was possible for privileged people to identify with him without feeling uncomfortable in their well-maintained suburban houses and in their solidarity with the established order. Romero was not, as Jesus was, dishonored and placed on a footing with outcasts and thieves. My aim here is obviously not to diminish the martyrdom of Archbishop Romero (a symbol of so many other obscure martyrdoms among the poor of his country) but to emphasize the scandal of Jesus' execution.

Nevertheless, this was the Jesus who, put to death

among thieves, rejected, a laughingstock, was raised up again by the Father, as told by the scriptures. Christians commemorate that death and resurrection in the Eucharist at the moment when they too celebrate decisions which they take in his memory, and their own confrontation with death.

Eucharist—more than a sharing

The Last Supper is much more than a sharing! Our society, and particularly its more privileged classes, like dwelling on this idea of sharing (the poor talk less about it but do more of it!). Sharing is seen as a balm in a hard and unjust socioeconomic situation. It softens social conflicts but, except when it attains a rare radicality, it does not affect the causes of injustice. Many eucharistic "sharings" end by accepting that, despite all the injustices, we are still capable of giving ourselves and of living together. These attitudes possess a genuine value. I believe, however, that they do not fully celebrate the specific story of him who was crucified, in that they refrain from indicating how Jesus was caught up in the conflicts generated by his actions. Christ is not simply a good man who calls upon us to share and to love humankind; he lives to the end, and in conflict, his trust in his Father and in human beings; he does not speak merely of love but of love for one's enemies. In that he is revelation.

The God revealed in Jesus Christ and celebrated in the Eucharist is, therefore, not just a loving God but a God who becomes so deeply involved in human tensions as to suffer, a God who is caught up in unsought human conflicts. In more theological terms, the incarnation is not just a proof of love but also a redeeming love, involved in the human reality of oppression and alienation, in brief, of sin. In the words of Sobrino: "The cross is the outcome of an incarnation in a world of sin marked out as a power which works against the God of Jesus." To say that Jesus dies because God wants him to die is inadequate; he dies in living to the end the conflict inherent in his testimony before a society (or rather a dominant class) which wants a God different from his. Jesus was condemned as an agitator, not because his action would be limited to that but because his love was concrete, in a real society, and therefore more political than idealistic. And if he is judged a blasphemer, it is because his God is quite different from the God adored by those who condemn him. The conflict which brought Jesus to death does not concern only an internal or mystical conception of salvation; it is the end result of a historical path in a specific society. That is why the eucharistic celebration cannot be reduced to a spiritual mysticism of the cross; it celebrates our concrete endeavors to follow the historical path of Jesus and sees in them the gift of God.

The Eucharist challenges

When the Eucharist truly commemorates Jesus crucified amid thieves it challenges the Christian community and questions it about the places where God is revealed today. It does not moralize, but helps participants to act out and to live the confrontation with the historical Jesus, who is always living in the people of God. Such a sacrament challenges our Christian communities, which often prefer to find their loyalties among "established people." Is it possible to celebrate the execution of one who was regarded as an agitator and to keep oneself separate from the "damned of the earth"? It would doubtless be pleasanter to picture only a resurrected Jesus reigning above the conflicts that shake society, and above all not a Jesus who is discredited in respected circles. It is also tempting to find theological explanations for the death of Jesus, without having to face the many and various ways in which he is put to death in our current society. On the contrary, the confrontation with Jesus' execution makes it necessary to look at those whom the established order (or disorder) is crushing and therefore to consider the sociopolitical dimension of the world's sin. Do we who celebrate the Eucharist really feel solidarity with him who was killed? What, in our society, does it mean to be in solidarity with him? How can we express this solidarity?

The death of Jesus is at the center of the Eucharist, for it sends Christians back to the historical conflicts in which they are situated. It shows them that it is in those conflicts and those crises—and not in the clouds—that one sees who God is and who the God of Jesus is. The execution of Jesus raises, with the seriousness of death and rejection, the question of our solidarity and that of the solidarity of God.

While the Eucharist is the celebration of the death of Jesus, it is also the celebration of hope, which refers to the action of the Father who raised Jesus up again. This hope, with the dimension of confidence and joy that it implies, enables Christians to follow the historical path of Jesus. This same hope is already being realized through the partial liberations being experienced by human beings. It is therefore important that, in the Eucharist, Christian communities should remember these liberations and celebrate them as a pledge of the resurrection.

Celebrations and their context

In the light of the foregoing, I shall examine traditional eucharistic rites and show how, through them, it is possible to live the mystery of the death and resurrection of Jesus and to discover how he delivers up his life in the sacrifice of himself which is liberating for all.

a. The liturgy of forgiveness. Eucharistic liturgies normally start with a celebration of forgiveness. This celebration is sometimes regarded as an aside, a sort of preamble which permits greater communion before the true eucharistic celebration. I believe this to be an error: Forgiveness appears to me to be the essential step which puts us in touch with the concrete conflicts of existence and therefore helps us to avoid living a "perverted" celebration.

The celebration of forgiveness at the beginning of the Eucharist commemorates our conflict-causing commitments. We are engaged in struggles; in these struggles it happens that we hurt and clash with people, and we ourselves are sometimes hurt. Workers, for instance, cannot conduct a strike without other workers or employers suffering thereby. A couple cannot make decisions without certain aspects of these decisions causing conflict. We have enemies; we are in pain ourselves. Moreover, we are not always convinced that we can be loved with our limitations and shortcomings. In order to celebrate the Eucharist and make the decisions which involve our lives, it is important not to let ourselves be imprisoned in these conflicts and clashes. Our enemies cannot be reduced purely to their part in our conflictive relationships. In other words, beyond and within these hard and sometimes painful situations, there is a place for tenderness, that attitude which transcends conflicts and humanizes them. Tenderness is request and acceptance, request and acceptance of forgiveness. Moreover, if we think about it, forgiveness was important at the Last Supper, for it was in conflict and in confrontation with enemies that Jesus delivered up his life. The celebration of forgiveness leads us to acknowledge the partly conflictive background of our own decisions, those which we are going to take in the footsteps of Jesus and which we will receive as the gift of God in our lives.

It is important to get in touch with these conflicts and to live them, remembering the forgiveness of God and human forgiveness. In this way we shall know that beyond the pains connected with the struggles there is room for us and for others; indeed, forgiveness is acceptance of the others as they are, with their limitations and situations. Forgiveness is asked, given and received without trying to determine who is right or wrong, nor how far. It does not do away with conflicts, but humanizes them. This was, I believe, the attitude of Jesus on the evening of the Last Supper. All the tenderness expressed there enabled him later to live and die as he did.

b. The Liturgy of the Word. The Liturgy of the Word traditionally contains two types of readings: the epistles (accounts of the practices and words of various Christian communities) and the gospel (accounts of the practices of and stands taken by Jesus). These readings bring the community face to face with words which it has not produced, which for it mean an "otherness," and which invite it not to close in on itself but to open itself to the word of God.

These readings prepare the community to face the question which will underlie the celebration: What are the practices and stands concerning which we shall say with Jesus: "Here is my life for you"? There is no point in dwelling at length here on the Liturgy of the Word, since it is properly lived in many Christian communities. Nevertheless, a pitfall must be pointed out. It may happen that, following the exchange, the community feels itself mobilized for a social action to be prepared in the immediate future, or that it wants to discuss, in greater detail, theoretical positions that have been brought up. These two practices are extremely useful but do not normally have their proper place in the celebration. Celebrating, in fact, is not doing something but "marking the event" symbolically and feeling the various meanings involved in our actions. Programming a social action is very important (sometimes more so than "celebrating") but it is different from a ritual feast with its own peculiar riches. Similarly, if a community discusses, for example, in order to understand a bible text exactly, this quest for accuracy and univocal meaning, useful as it may be, runs counter to the multiple meanings characteristic of symbolic language. Analysis of texts in order to bring out the meanings and the conflicts which they express may help to prevent a community from projecting its own ideology too much into scripture. The Liturgy of the Word, however, is aimed neither at determining an action to be done (this would once again be a way of moralizing) nor at producing a correct argument, but at listening through the texts to the word of God, in order to see how it affects our lives and choices today. At the end of the Liturgy of the Word lies a profession of faith, a symbolic act in which the community acknowledges itself to be touched by the word of God.

    c. Intentions and the Preparation of the Gifts. Next comes the prayer of the faithful: The community recalls situations—both near and distant—which it will carry into the celebration. This part gives content to the Eucharist and relates it to daily life. Stories are told in which people are in situations similar to that in which Jesus found himself on the evening of the Last Supper; people often face tensions and conflicts in which they are going to be involved, without knowing exactly where they are going.

Where the community celebrates choices that have a special meaning for it (we may consider the example of the nuns who decided to resign from the hospital where they worked), it is necessary to mention what each person bears in his or her heart, whether this refers to individual or to collective situations.

In these petitions, persons presiding over and/or conducting the Eucharist have an important task: to evoke situations of which the community does not think automatically and which appear foreign to it. It is necessary to ensure that the community does not turn into a sect concerned only with itself. Testimonies and intentions must therefore refer to what is often forgotten, in particular to the struggles for justice lived by groups or social classes to which the community does not feel itself to be in direct proximity. Some of these reminders could even be painful (for example, a strike in a mainly middle-class area); it is nevertheless the task of those conducting the Eucharist to echo the life of the universal church and to show how God is found in places other than those familiar to the group that is celebrating. Moreover, this group will celebrate fruitfully only if it can come into contact with its own contradictions and limitations.

The presentation of the symbols of bread and wine, "fruit of the vine and work of human hands," can, in its own turn, help people face life and its contradictions. Bread and wine are indeed signs; they evoke sharing, the gathered grain, life, exchanged tenderness; the joy of sharing from the same cup what the human community has been able to produce. They also refer to the reality of conflicts in life. Bread is fought for and human beings are exploited in order to produce what others will consume. The grapes for wine in our modern society, in particular, are generally harvested by migrant workers who are often exploited and deprived of elementary rights. Bread and wine can thus be symbols of what is lived; Christian hope also sees in them the possibility of becoming the "bread of life" and "the cup of salvation."

d. The Eucharistic Prayer. The Eucharistic Prayer begins with the prayer of thanksgiving. This is important.

Before evoking the mystery of death, it is necessary to be able to say what life is and what today reveals to us the mystery of God. This alternating between the tensions and joys of our existence will, in fact, give texture to the rite. The gifts received will open the way to a symbolic language which will recognize the giver and the mystery of God's love.

Next the Eucharistic Prayer commemorates Jesus. It recalls his actions, the people he cured, his liberating words, the conflicts which they provoked, and finally how that led him to Holy Thursday. Remembering the moment when he knew that he was not going to escape and was going to die—at least if he continued to bear witness to the liberating love of his Father—the liturgy speaks of the blessing he gave. This blessing is often mentioned and forgotten too quickly. Yet to bless is to remember the love of the Father and to believe that what comes is the gift of God. Jesus therefore remembered the love of his Father who, since baptism, had never abandoned him. In trust, he discovered and welcomed his present situation as a gift from God. Then, once again, faced with the unknown, he placed his trust in his Father; he took the bread, shared it and said: "Here is my life for you." The translation, "This is my body," is doubtless in the end less faithful than that which speaks of the gift of life. We Westerners are accustomed to the biological body, to the dead body, separated from the presence which it manifests; we have a tendency to understand "This is my body" in a much too materialistic fashion. What Jesus delivers up is nothing other than himself, his life, his Real Presence as expressed in theology, and not his body understood as separated from him. The same applies to the sharing of the blood. In the words of the institution, it is mentioned that it will be shed "for the remission of sins." A purely individualistic conception of the remission of sins is inadequate. The concern is not for only personal sins but also the sin of the world, all the alienations and exploitations which are present in humankind. The "remission of sins" aims both at the forgiveness of God and at the establishment of a kingdom in which mutual forgiveness becomes possible.

Perhaps a good way of suggesting it would be to say: "in order that human beings may live forgiveness," or "in order that human beings may forgive one another." If Jesus gives his life, it is in connection with his commitment that the kingdom may come: a new mode of existence, linked to the God of Jesus, the God of forgiveness and liberation, the God who does neither measure nor remember debts but gives unconditionally.

e. By my Spirit, do as I did in memory of me. An initial interpretation of these words sees them as an invitation to repeat the rite. There is more, however; beyond the rite lies the call to accomplish the reality evoked: "Whenever you too are called upon to deliver up your life, remember me and do as I did." In this sense, the invitation is to do as Jesus did, that is, to deliver up one's life in trust as he did. Insofar as Christians relive in their existence the actions, conflicts, passion and death of Jesus they participate in his resurrection and await his coming.

In order to live thus, Christians must be imbued with the Spirit of Jesus. They need him in order to be able to say, in all the situations previously mentioned, "Here is my life, for you." That is why the liturgy quite naturally prays for the community to receive the Spirit. Next it describes the powerful action of that Spirit, which renews the face of the earth. Through it people choose their solidarity with the oppressed; they are concerned for the weak; they succeed in standing on their own feet; they are full of tenderness, wisdom and openness; they pull down the oppressive barriers between master and slave, heathen and Jew, man and woman; they discover themselves in communion as brothers and sisters: pope, clergy, strong, weak, bishops, different races, etc. It should not be a hollow or false reconciliation but the proclamation and hope that, through the Spirit of Jesus, something other than conflict is in the process of being born and that new relationships, a new heaven and a new earth, are coming forth. Through Jesus, in him and with him, all honor and glory are then rendered to the Father.

f. The feast of communion. Tradition then invites the community to say the Lord's Prayer, exchange the sign of peace, and share the bread of life and the chalice of salvation, the body and blood of Jesus. The communion feast is the feast of the hope of Christians that through all the encounters, struggles, joys and pains, conflicts and forgiveness of existence, the kingdom of God, of sharing love and communion, will arise. After a period of silence which will enable all that has been experienced to be absorbed and which will reflect the individual and collective manner of following Jesus, the rite finishes with a prayer and/or a hymn of thanksgiving, a thanksgiving to God and, more tangibly, to the others with whom one has celebrated.

Conclusion: Perversions of the Eucharist

After reflecting on the eucharistic celebration, let us examine how it can be, and often has been, turned from its original purpose. I shall dwell on four ways, among many others.

First, the Eucharist is perverted, in my view, when it no longer celebrates the concrete death of Jesus giving up his life and put in the same class with thieves. This distortion occurs when the Eucharist is presented as a simple religious sacrifice and/or worship without reference to the way in which Jesus gave his life.

It is also distorted when it has no specific content, i.e., when the rite does not refer to the way in which, in both a social and individual context, the community lives its tensions, choices and options, and feels itself called upon to deliver up its life, remembering Jesus.

The same applies when the content of the celebration is made a private matter, referring only to the individual and his inner life, and no longer to the whole of society.

Finally, the "perversion" seems to me to be greatest when the Eucharist is celebrated in order to mark a commitment, options or social choices opposed to those of Jesus. Although it is always difficult to judge in actual practice what is opposed to the loyalties of Jesus, celebrations for certain revolutions, or again celebrations by ruling classes which do not wish to recognize their contradictions, can, in my opinion, rightly be regarded as sacrileges.

The last "perversion" shows how for Christians the Eucharist can be an ethical criterion. In the Eucharist Christians take their lives and their choices in hand and say, in the footsteps of Jesus and in memory of him, "Here is my life, for you." It may happen that the community or individuals feel that it would be incongruous, even scandalous, to celebrate the Eucharist around certain choices—to choose to exploit the poor, for example. Where the Christian community considers it inconceivable to celebrate the Eucharist in connection with certain options, one may say that these options are contrary to Christian ethics.

4 | Baptism: Liberated or Crushed by Human Community

Baptism celebrates the welcoming of a new member into the Christian community that is the church. As in the case of every sacrament, reflection may be undertaken in two ways: either on the basis of the traditions which summon us to celebrate this rite, or on the basis of the specific human situations which might be celebrated. Chronologically, religious or simply cultural traditions are always first; they provide readings of concrete reality which determine what should be celebrated and which indicate (sometimes very badly) tensions in connection with which it is worth "marking the occasion."

The human tensions underlying baptism

What are the human tensions underlying baptism? They are those evoked by a person's entry into a new group and the discovery of a new type of relationship; they constitute a passage and a sort of rebirth. Birth can be defined in cultural terms as the entry into a tissue of human relations; to be welcomed into a community is a way of restructuring or renewing this network of human relations and, therefore, is indeed a new birth.

Reception into the church occurs either in adulthood or in early childhood. The celebration cannot be the same for both adults and children. As the baptism of children is the most common type of baptism, I shall speak primarily of this celebration; adjustments will have to be made for an adult.

The appearance of a new member upsets relationships in the group and changes its structure. In the case of a child, the change in family relationships is especially profound. If it is the first child, its birth will affect mainly the parents; in the case of subsequent children, their brothers and sisters also feel the difference. These changes are not always lived through easily; the parents are compelled to reorganize their use of time and even their emotional life because of their child. Older children often experience the birth of a small brother or sister as an intrusion. Even independently of any religious tradition, it is important to take time to live through these changes; these changes must be expressed in the rite, on pain of distorting the celebration. Families which do not "mark the occasion" risk feeling an uneasiness which will last as long as they have not incorporated the change.

One of the reasons for celebrating a baptism is therefore to take time to feel all the changes introduced by the coming of the new member. The child's entry into the group elicits questions: What place will be given to it? What experience will be had with the child? Will it be accepted and loved, or rejected? The new presence will bring conflicts since, after all, one begins to live genuinely with someone only when it is felt that that person is wrenching us away from our routines. At that moment, the person concerned appears truly "other," different from us. A new question then arises for the receiving group: Will this community be for this person a place where he or she will be able to breathe, a place where God's love will be revealed and where, in the end, God will be made visible? In this way, starting from the reception of the new member, more radical questions will gradually arise which will open the way to the whole mystery of salvation.

Nearly all parents ask these questions, at least in some confused way. Their hopes for the child are great, but these hopes stand out against a background of fears, for the parents know that the world is cruel and overpowering. It is not only a community where all love one another but also—perhaps primarily?—a society of oppression, exploitation and alienation (in traditional theological terms: a society historically marked by original sin). The parents also have questions about themselves. They wonder if they will be capable of giving their child its independence or if they will try to possess him or her and impose their own ways. They also wonder to what extent the child will be influenced by their limitations—psychological, financial, social, etc.—and by societal organization. From the beginning of its existence the child is already marked by limitations. These are not only inevitabilities but are also the result of a historical system: the presence of evil in society and in individual evolution.

The mystery of evil, and hope

The mystery of evil has been symbolized in Christian traditions by the doctrine of original sin. According to this doctrine, human beings live in a community in which people are oppressed by people, a community of "sin"; and this oppression historically affects the whole human community to such an extent that individuals are marked to their innermost depths. This traditional doctrine does not describe a purely individual situation (as with the image of a stain on "my" soul) but refers primarily to a collective situation which touches individuals in their inmost beings. One is affected by this mystery of evil simply by being a member of the human community. The traditional doctrine sedulously avoided presenting this mystery as an eternal destiny; on the contrary, original sin was presented as historical, linked to Adam and Eve. The doctrine of original sin therefore invites us to seek in human history the mechanisms through which the society of sin or oppression has been (and still is being) constructed. In other words, this tradition invites us to see how, historically, social (as well as economic, family and political) systems affect individuals in their inmost selves.

This coincides, moreover, with the approach adopted by psychoanalysis when it considers the way in which parental conflicts fashion the psychology of children. It notes, for instance, how difficult it is in a patriarchal society to establish a true partnership between a woman and a man. There are consequences of history for which no one is individually responsible but with which every person is deeply imbued. The same applies to work relationships and to exploitation in a materialist world, where everyone lives on exploitation and suffers its consequences without failing to be to some extent a party to it. These alienations and many others which Christian traditions have called the "consequences of original sin" are felt, at least in confused fashion, by the parents, relatives and friends of a newborn child.

In short, the welcoming of a new member into a community always takes place against a background linked to an oppressive society; at the same time, baptism is celebrated in the face of a humanity touched by original sin. In both cases, symbolic language speaks of an alienation which affects all human beings, which is not the outcome of chance or of some inevitability, but which is indeed the result of historical human actions, an alienation in short for which no one is individually responsible but to which each person is, to some extent, a party. It is against this background that Christian hope has its meaning.

Described in an abstract manner, the sin of the world and the oppressive society may seem to be intellectual concepts remote from the actual life of a community which welcomes a child. To make these ideas more specific, it is sufficient to put a very simple question to parents and relatives: What are your fears regarding the future of this child? The replies will generally be: "That the child will not be able to do what it wants to do"; "that we will impose our own ideas and attitudes on the child so that it will be prevented from living"; "that he will find himself out of work like so many others"; "that her health will be bad"; "that at school she will have teachers who will destroy her originality"; "that in religion classes he will be given ideas which have little to do with the gospel of Jesus Christ"; "that he will be recruited into a state, a political party, a business, or a church which will use him for its own ends"; "that he will be forced to fight in a war"; "that she will not succeed in learning how to love"; etc. If the community is allowed to express itself, it will very accurately describe the oppressions in our society.

The community of the kingdom

How can we get out of this alienation? The Christian response is simple: God awakens his kingdom among women and men, that is, a community where forgiveness and tenderness reign, thanks to the unconditional love of God and of those who follow in the footsteps of Jesus. God thus establishes his justice, a liberation from all oppressions. This liberation touches much more than an "inner life"; it affects all that is human: bodies and spirits, individuals, groups, organizations and communities.

The assembly of the faithful (the church) is now trying to live this kingdom. When it celebrates its existence, it refers to this gift of God, to come but already present: the kingdom of justice, of love, the kingdom of forgiveness and the gracious gift of God. Christian communities thus see themselves as places where the liberation of God is proclaimed, where it is in action. But this liberation, in a society and church still inhabited by injustice, is never completely achieved. The celebration of the church, its existence as a sacrament, consists in celebrating, in this ambiguous situation, the hope which dwells in it. There are, of course, many "places of liberation" outside the church; it does not have a monopoly on them!

Here again, this idea of a liberating community must not be left in the abstract. The person conducting the celebration may ask: "What are the actions which we are undertaking in order to struggle against injustice and build the kingdom?" There, too, replies may vary. Parents, for example, will explain that they do not wish to possess their children but, on the contrary, to create for them conditions of freedom. Social activists will speak of specific actions on behalf of oppressed or exploited groups. Others will relate the struggles undertaken against bureaucracies. Likewise, religious renewals and the way in which the faithful labor to change the church's structures also testify to places where hope may be born. Mention of the men and women who have given their lives in the struggle for justice will reveal, with respect to the new member of the community, the power of God which tends to transform all things.

Baptism as the acting out of a passage

Baptism is aimed at celebrating (i.e., ritually acting out) a passage or transition which is never totally achieved and which nevertheless takes place unceasingly; it recognizes in this passage the action of the liberating God. Its purpose is to communicate the reality that, when one discovers a community where forgiveness, tenderness and justice are already lived, one is emerging from the world of sin, being purified and born again.

The accounts of the deliverance from Egypt and the crossing of the Red Sea have traditionally been used to evoke this liberation. In Egypt, the people of God were Pharaoh's slaves, the slaves of all the structures of oppression which governed the country. Going out of Egypt, the Hebrews reached a place where they could live as a free people. This founding account clearly symbolizes the tension between the hope of the community and the analysis of the oppressions conveyed in societies and psychologies; it has become the foremost symbol of the liberating God.

The action of a community

From this viewpoint baptism may be described principally as the act of a community summoned by God to be, for the new member, a concrete manifestation of his love. The rite will be linked to the awareness by the community that God's love can become visible through its concrete action in human history. The rite will bear its fruit if the members of the community emerge from it more determined to be for one another a community of liberation (a church) assembled by God with a view to his kingdom.

It is, moreover, in this way that baptism can be said to confer faith, for to live faith is to trust in God's love powerfully revealed in the people. The sacramental rite confers faith insofar as it transforms the community by causing it to realize that it can achieve the liberations which will make God's action visible. Faith is not conferred by some magical mechanism but by what the new member can feel, touch and experience, by discovering God's power at work in society. "To live faith" is to place oneself in the traditions of those who have recognized God through the liberating action they have experienced and celebrated.

The very words of baptism may be understood from this viewpoint of liberation from human oppressions. In a society where people stick their claws into one another, it is important to affirm that a human being is the property of no one. That is the meaning of the proclamation: "I baptize you in the name of the Father, Son and Holy Spirit." The new member is not baptized in the name of his or her family, parents, a political party, clan or ethnic group or social class, but in the name of God. This is something quite different. The new member becomes a child of God and of no one else. This reference to God (who lays hands on no one) is clarified by the scene in the gospel where the clan of Jesus tries to "win him back," to "bring him back to reason," to take him back to "his place," in Nazareth; to this Jesus replies: "My mother, my brother—they are those who hear the word of God and act upon it" (Lk 8:21). Previously, as Luke tells us, he had slipped away from his parents so as to be "about my Father's business." There again is found the tension between a society which wishes to possess its members and the liberty proclaimed in the name of God.

Celebrating hope in an oppressive society

For baptism to help the community get in touch with what it lives, the rite must bring some awareness of the tensions which are related to this celebration. In this way, as noted above, everyone will be brought, by readings or discussions, to a better grasp of the reality of the "sin of the world" in our society. It will be a good idea to spell out what threatens the new member and the whole community: collective oppressions, war, injustices, the daily rat race, psychological limitations, family tensions, etc. Then one can consider the tensions caused by the appearance of the new member. If it is a child, the whole reorganization of the parents' life should be mentioned; if it is an adult, the latter's own culture and history will be part of what the community will have to take into account.

The entry of the new member into the community confronts the latter with the various tensions symbolized by the concept of original sin; but the viewpoint is one of hope. There are not only oppressions; those who put Jesus to death are not the only ones who count. Christians also affirm the resurrection of Jesus and the action of all those who, in his footsteps, have learned to stand upright. The celebration will therefore express the effects of liberation and the signs of salvation, and they are many.

The solidarity of the community

The contrast between human oppression and the hope of salvation challenges the community celebrating baptism: Where does it (the community) stand? Its look at human history faces it with a fundamental query and compels it to make choices of solidarity. In the liturgies of baptism these choices were, until recently, symbolized by the question: "Do you renounce Satan?" In modern symbolism, however, this question has become for many people a strange one for, on the one hand, the meaning of Satan has often been lost and, on the other hand, the question appears highly moralizing. But today, in other forms, we continue to wonder, perhaps even more urgently: What will we be for the new member? Will we be the community that testifies to the gracious and unconditional love of God? Or, on the contrary, will we be accomplices in human oppression? The question, "Do you renounce Satan and all his works?" is the same as asking, "What is the situation we choose in history, the stake of which is God's justice?" The question must not be presented so as to produce feelings of guilt, for one remains party to a world of sin and oppression; but it points to a radical choice in existence, the choice which was central to the practices of Jesus. The Christian community, salvation and the liberation which is its sign, are not given automatically; they are the stake of a struggle for justice in which God takes sides on behalf of the oppressed in the face of the forces of evil, traditionally represented by Satan. There is no Christian community—and therefore no baptism—without this reference; it is what was proclaimed by the international Synod of Bishops in 1971; "Action on behalf of justice and participation in the transformation of the world fully appears to us as a constitutive dimension of the preaching of the gospel, or, in other words, of the church's mission for the redemption of the human race and its liberation from every oppressive situation." It is not a question of casting blame or of moralizing but of indicating the stakes of the history of salvation.

A light in the world

The symbolism of baptism uses the light of the paschal candle: Amid the shadows of the night appears a light linked to the resurrection of Jesus. At a time when, by his condemnation, his torture and death, Jesus appeared wholly subject to the forces of darkness, behold, God had not abandoned him and hope has gained the upper hand. The disciples of Emmaus also had the impression that all was lost, and here, once again, the light is with them. The same applies to the Christian community and its new member: Ceaselessly confronting oppression, sin in all its forms, and death, it finds its hope in faith in this liberating action of God, symbolized by Jesus' resurrection. Of course, this commemoration of the resurrection of Jesus following his passion will be full of meaning only if the community can be the light of Christ for its new member.

The symbolisms of water and immersion speak of being plunged into life and death, of the transition of rebirth, and of the new freshness which are linked to bathing. They evoke the liberating crossing of the Red Sea. Entering a community of love can change the whole of existence. Diving into water is a way of acting out what one hopes for from God: We are all plunged into the mystery of evil in order to be reborn in a new community.

The "perversions" of baptism

The sacrament of baptism can easily be perverted, i.e., used not for the liberation of human beings but instead for their being taken over by established societal structures (whether these are civil or ecclesiastical).

The "perversion" most strongly felt today is undoubtedly the tendency to consider baptism as a taking over of the new member by the church. A fairly common practice tended in this direction. Did not canon law go so far as to state that the church has rights over the newly baptized and that from the moment it formed part of the Christian community it was subject to its law? Although these statements can be interpreted positively, it has to be recognized that, in a clerical and often guilt-producing church, membership in the Christian community is not always "good news." When certain celebrations of baptism express the taking over of the new member by the "sect of Christians," one is in the presence of a "perverted" sacrament. Thus, for some parents, baptism—and what it seems to imply—is a problem. Religion classes, wrongly identified with Christian education, do not all communicate the good news of Jesus. And while the gospel is liberating, the thinking of the catechist is not always so. In a church that sometimes oppresses consciences, Christians hesitate to have their children baptized for fear of allowing their liberty to be violated.

In the face of these fears, it is important to spell out at baptism that the new member is not entering into a community belonging to any particular type of person, clergy, bishop or pope but into the community of Jesus Christ who does not want to possess anyone. Without this clarification there is a risk of confusing the hope of the kingdom with tangible institutions which are sometimes products of alienation and the sin of the world.

From the same viewpoint, the sacrament of baptism is distorted when the new member is made to pass a sort of individual examination and is asked whether he or she has faith and renounces Satan. Such an attitude masks the theme of the celebration, namely, the gratuitous gift of God in the face of the radical question of sin in the world. This sin is not, moreover, an individual state in the first place but a situation in which we are all immersed. To attach a moral or guilt to access to the kingdom is to distort its nature; the kingdom is the gracious gift of God, his grace, the very gift making it possible, in him, to build a community of love.

When the baptism of children is considered in this way, numerous difficulties which it raises begin to fade. What problem is there, indeed, in celebrating the fact that one wants to share with one's children the hope on which one lives, provided, however, that this entry into the Christian community does not mean that the baptized member has to move with a ball and chain attached? The baptism of children must always, therefore, affirm that in the end they themselves will have to decide their lives; if the practices of the Christian community were one day to become an obstacle for them ("an object of scandal"), it would be quite reasonable and fitting for them to leave it.

Finally, one last "perversion" of baptism appears to me to be fairly common. I am thinking of those celebrations in which the new member is welcomed as if society was unaware of any problem and as if no oppression, no tension, no "original sin" existed. This kind of rite presents a society without conflicts in which everyone is nice and kind. Baptism then emerges as a celebration which denies reality and suggests that one can protect oneself against it. At the time such a celebration may be extremely pleasant, like those psychological methods by which we persuade ourselves that everything is going right. But many people know that this is not true; it is only a way—often unconscious—of avoiding reality and its tensions. That is why a feeling of peace is only rarely derived from such celebrations. Peace comes when one celebrates the contradictions of life and not when one avoids them; it comes in the celebration of existence as it is and not of existence as a protected group wishes to imagine it. In Christian terms, peace is considered authentic only if it has been steeped in the solidarity of him who was killed in his confrontation with evil and whom the Father raised up.

5 | Confirmation: New Voices in the Community

Many nowadays propose that the age of confirmation be delayed because they consider that young people should have reached a certain maturity if they are to be committed persons. Popular imagery and theology depict confirmation as the sacrament of commitment; through it one becomes a "soldier of Christ," promises to act on behalf of the faith and the church, and renews baptismal vows. This sacrament is usually lived as the rite of full integration in the church, viewed as an established community; through it the Christian becomes a complete member of the church and will participate more deeply in its life. From this it follows that thinking concerning confirmation is often highly moralizing: It specifies what the community expects of the individual now that he or she is a full member. This explains the impression of many young (and not so young) people that this sacrament is a taking over of the confirmed person by the church. If the former is ready to commit himself in the church people will find it reasonable for him to be confirmed; but many will often add that the confirmed person is very young to get involved in this way. They will also wonder whether it is reasonable to enter into such a commitment for life when no one can control the future.

In short, the rite of confirmation and its preparation are often seen as an attempt by the institution to take over young people and new members. Such a view appears to me to be a distortion of the sacrament since it is hard to reconcile it with the celebration of a gracious gift of God; far from wishing to take over young people or adults, God calls everyone to be free.

Tensions with respect to the new member

A community is always slightly anxious in the face of its new members since they will bring with them a breath of fresh air and new ideas. If they are adult, they will have lived other experiences and traditions; if they are young[1], they will challenge many routines. That is why the community is often tempted to control them by asking them to involve themselves in accordance with the community's own idea of what they should be.

This is a special temptation for parents; do they not, too often, desire their children to be carbon copies of them? On the other hand, they are easily put off when young people adopt directions that differ from theirs; in such cases, they feel challenged. Many of them are therefore afraid of this period when their children take their independence.

The church too sometimes fears new members and especially the young; it then succumbs to the temptation to propose oversimplistic images of what a "good committed Christian" is, as if it were possible to say in advance where the Spirit will lead people. Hence the ideology of "commitment" is stressed in connection with confirmation.

With regard to new members, their fear is often just as genuine since what they are committing themselves to is new. Acquiring a say in matters and assuming responsibility does not take place without tension. In every society, such tension is the subject of initiation rites, the aim of which is to exorcise the fear of the unknown and to master the new situation. In some cultures initiation is aimed at controlling the new member, at indicating the limits of what may be done and of penalizing any deviation. The freedom often allowed to children then ends with initia-

1. Here again I will emphasize the confirmation of young people, which is nowadays the most common. What is said can also be applied to adult new members coming with their past history and their own culture.

tion; when they are adults, they must submit to the commandments and prohibitions of the group. In other cases, initiation may be the celebration of novelty and of welcome for the unexpected. In any case, however, it is a moment when the group confronts novelty and tames it in order either to control it, set it free, or negotiate with it. When the sacrament of confirmation is lived in the ideology of commitment, it seems to come under the first tendency, that of control. But when one takes seriously theological thinking concerning the Spirit, this same sacrament may be the rite of welcome of the Spirit, of which one knows neither the origin nor the destination.

From its beginnings the church has wondered about the attitude it should take to newcomers and about the way to recognize the Spirit which they have received. The gentiles very quickly shook the church, which was initially composed of Jews. Peter thus had to review his values: Chapter 10 of the Acts shows him agreeing to eat so-called impure food and rubbing elbows with gentiles. The text attributes this change to the bursting in of the Spirit: "Peter was still speaking when the Holy Spirit came upon all who were listening to the message. The believers who had come with Peter, men of Jewish birth, were astonished that the gift of the Holy Spirit should have been poured out *even on gentiles*" (Acts 10:44-45). A similar astonishment seizes many adults in the face of the new generations: They find it hard to believe that these too have received the Spirit. Likewise, the churches in the industrialized countries are often dumbfounded to see that the Spirit speaks differently in the developing countries. Nevertheless, the irruption of the Spirit is an event that forces communities to become open to attitudes which they would otherwise have rejected; it is generally neophytes, less accustomed to routine, who indicate new paths in which the church recognizes the mark of the Spirit, sometimes after some hesitation.

Celebrating the new voice in the community

From the above viewpoint, we can outline a vision of the human experience at which the sacrament of confirmation is aimed. It consists of a confrontation with new full members. This confrontation implies a restructuring of the community as the newcomer will acquire a say and power in the group. Acquisition of a say and power should be celebrated, as should all that creates social bonds. Such new bonds—in theological language, this new presence of the Spirit—are both desired and feared. They are ambiguous in nature: Some are sources of joy but all bring tensions, for they herald a change in the previous balance, which is always a little frightening. The sacrament of confirmation celebrates in this change the gracious gift of the Spirit of God; this gift is expressed in the say acquired by the new member, in the intrusion and even the aggression of that member.

The affirmation, traditionally central to this sacrament, that "in it Christians receive the Spirit" implies that they have something original to say and that they must be taken seriously. In their word must be recognized one of the ways in which the Spirit speaks to the community. Would not the celebrating of confirmation mean, then, taking into account the words and actions of the persons confirmed? Would it not be a celebration of the place accorded to young people (or to new adult members)? Would not having and receiving the Spirit mean quite simply having one's own voices in matters and performing actions not determined by the group to which one belongs? And no one knows whence this Spirit comes nor whither it goes; it blows as a tempest with the ardor of youth. That is why we need rites and feasts to confront its irruption, to live both its strength and tenderness. Such a viewpoint is practically the opposite of compliance and enrollment in a group; the issue is to know whether, and how far, the community is going to accept its new member as a person to be listened to, who has something to say and do, in whom the Spirit gives utterance and who, in the end, will follow his or her own path.

Take seriously the Spirit in everyone

Christian communities have difficulty in taking seriously the Spirit which all the faithful have received.

Too often the church has adopted the attitude of civil societies, which are convinced that only experts or people of a certain social level deserve to be heard. Yet the best established Christian traditions stress that the Spirit of God speaks through all persons and all social groups. It speaks through the poor and the young just as much as through the rich and the old. It speaks through both men and women, through the just and through "sinners," through simple people and through scholars and experts, through every Christian and through bishops, through workers and through theologians, through foreigners and through natives, etc. Affirming in this way the sovereign independence of the Spirit with respect to our divisions does not mean that we are ignoring differences in functions; but Christian traditions state that over and beyond these diversities everyone shares in the same Spirit.

Taking seriously the Spirit who speaks through all the members of the church has profound ecclesiological repercussions which may, moreover, be evoked at the celebration of confirmation. There are not two churches, one teaching and possessing the Spirit, and the other taught and listening to the Spirit coming from elsewhere. The whole church is both taught and teaching. Nor is it correct to believe that only the hierarchy has the task of testifying to the faith of the apostles; the whole church testifies to it, and the task of keeping the evangelical message intact is fulfilled by the Christian community as a whole. Some practice a more specific church ministry related to the transmission of the traditions of faith (what is called the magisterium of bishops), but the task of conveying the evangelical message to the world and preserving its authenticity belongs to the whole church and not just to the first mentioned. As regards the bishops, their role in the magisterium is to bear witness to the faith of their churches and to the Spirit's action in them. Through their communities (their churches) they have a special perception of faith; their ministry and charisma is of the church. It could perhaps be said that their presence at the celebration of confirmation matters not so much to confer the sacrament but to symbolize, as bishops, that the whole church listens to the Spirit in the new members; and perhaps "conferring the sacrament" is mainly that listening ministry.

Confirmation may thus be considered the sacrament of the church community listening to the Spirit given to each member, especially the new members. In Chapter 12 of his gospel Luke shows Jesus warning the crowds against the leaven of the Pharisees and calling upon them not to resort always to experts and authorities in order to solve their problems: "And why can you not judge for yourselves what is the right course?" A church in which the Spirit speaks is quite the opposite of a consumer society or a programmed society, where nobody can speak without permission. It is not always easy to take seriously the Spirit which speaks in a Christian community. The Spirit indeed often reveals itself as an intruder. It causes conflicts which take time to resolve: The kingdom is like a field in which wheat and chaff grow together until the day when it will be possible to separate them. While recognizing the Spirit in all men and women, it will be necessary to be discerning, a task which, however, will never be completed.

Celebrating becoming an adult

Confirmation of the young must reflect the tensions and conflicts involved in reaching adulthood; young people begin to say what they are and what they live, while the community is shaken and disturbed by the intrusion of a new voice and a new way of doing things. As soon as young people approach adolescence, their parents wonder what their situation will be when the children begin to have ideas of their own. Will the new generation demolish the principles by which their parents lived? Will adults find words with which to help the young articulate their experiences? The young too ask themselves questions in the face of the ideologies of their parents; they see their limitations but when they go forward and expose themselves to new experiences they are unsure of themselves. They sometimes find it hard to believe in themselves. In the presence of all these hesitations, it is worthwhile celebrating gradually becoming an adult and the restructuring of the community it implies.

When should young people be confirmed?

Insofar as confirmation is regarded as the sacrament of commitment, the answer to this oft-put question is a difficult one. At what moment, indeed, can it be said that a young person, or even an adult, is mature enough to be able to commit his or her life? Moreover, up to what point is it honest to involve young people in a commitment which statistics say is a precarious one? Viewed thus, there is no simple answer to this question, which generally leads to the proposal that the age of confirmation be delayed.

However, if confirmation consists in celebrating the gift of God constituted by the Spirit that speaks through the new members of the community, the reply is simpler. In this case, the celebration does not imply a commitment in which the young people will later feel trapped; there will be a welcome at this sacrament for all those who are ready to celebrate the Spirit which they have received and are receiving. The gift is truly free with no kind of blackmail into a commitment. To be validly received, the sacrament of confirmation therefore requires nothing more than the other sacraments do: a desire to receive in good faith the gift of God in conjunction with the celebration of the church. There are no strings attached!

The gift of God in confirmation

Here, as for all the sacraments, the gift of God is powerfully revealed through the Christian community (the church). When people discover a community which takes them seriously and which listens to them while recognizing the Spirit in what they say, they can believe in the Spirit's presence in themselves. People are "confirmed" and changed by the fact that the community actually *listens*. Without this, it is difficult for them to believe that the Spirit of God is in them. One of the effects of the community's taking the new member seriously is undoubtedly that the latter too will pay special heed and will reflect on what he or she will say to the community and society.

Thus, what makes the sacrament efficacious is the faith and trust of the community (the church) in the Spirit which acts concretely in it. A community in which everyone listens to the others in seeking manifestations of the Spirit in them soon discovers that the Spirit speaks through each one, often in unexpected ways.

This listening to the Spirit may turn out to be the opposite: It is not unusual for communities to censure the diversity of voices speaking out by emphasizing that the Spirit speaks with one voice. Then, instead of welcoming an ever-new Spirit, these communities compel their members to say only the pious words that are expected of them. On the contrary, the sacrament in truth celebrates the confrontation between the new voice which is to be taken seriously and the routine of the established community. This intrusion of the Spirit is celebrated ritually, for it is hard to see how the mystery of the irruption of the new into the old can be expressed in any other way.

Toward an authentic feast of becoming a full member

A celebration of arrival at adulthood and of the gift of the Spirit is not improvised; like all feasts, it is prepared. The preparation is, first of all, for the young; in a society which regards them as infantile it is not easy for them to believe that one day they may be taken seriously and that their words and actions have importance. It matters that they hear stories which will make them realize that their links with adult society will change. They must also gradually see that they are going to shake the preceding generation. They should learn to consider the message which they are bringing to adult society as positive and as the expression of the Spirit which is in them, without ignoring the fact that this Spirit also speaks in adults. Finally, and above all, they must meet adults who take them seriously. That is why preparation of the adult community and parents is even more necessary; it is not so easy for them to take young people seriously, to listen to them, to persuade themselves that the new generation has a message for them and that it is capable of accepting its responsibilities—in short, in religious language, that God's

Spirit is in them. It is all the more difficult for them because our society gives little help to adults to see young people as nearly equal partners.

Preparation for confirmation should lead the whole community to celebrate the establishment of new social links between the young and grownups. The arrival of young people at adulthood restructures community and family relations; it is this that must be expressed in a celebration, in seeing in their arrival a gift of the Spirit. This gift assumes its meaning only against the background of a society and of individuals who aspire to liberation in the face of human oppression and exploitation. For the feast not to be a lie, it has to introduce this new social bond. The community must become aware and express in a ritual way the fact that it is situated *differently* with respect to the new member and that it considers the new member as *another* who has his or her own voice.

With regard to the new member, the latter could express in the feast who he or she is and what way of taking a place in the community is envisaged. In the celebration new members could say what they consider important. The aim is not to ask the new member to utter commitments or promises but—adults and young people—to live together the seriousness of adult existence between partners, knowing that each person contains both the Spirit and the world of sin. For the celebration to be a genuine one, it will therefore be necessary for the community to give a true place to the newcomer's specific voice, to listen to it, to distinguish it and to agree to learn from it. The celebration will thus refer the whole community to questions about the way it lives in society: How are persons treated? Is it with respect for their otherness? Or are they completely taken over by the socioeconomic system?

Conclusion

The celebration of the sacrament of confirmation therefore marks out the value of each person through whom the Spirit comes, as an intruder, who will renew the face of the earth. In the case of the confirmation of young people it is also the feast of the age-old confrontation of the generations, with all that this implies. The rites and preparation of the sacrament can effectively help the community to live peacefully this transition and this change in social relationships. They can help all the people concerned to face the mystery of the acquisition of a voice in matters with strength and gentleness and to recognize therein a manifestation of God.

6 | Penance: Celebration of Forgiveness in the Midst of Conflicts

Forgiveness is an attitude linked to several types of conflict-causing conditions: individual and collective relationships, the "violence" of transgressions, sin. Before considering the celebration of forgiveness, we will analyze some of the various approaches to the conflicts of existence.

The human condition is full of conflicts

Tensions and conflicts are ever present in life. Even if in our innermost being we long for complete peace, the reality is different. Whether we like it or not, we spend a great part of our life in conflicts; if we waited for them to be resolved before we accepted and loved our lives, we should wait forever. It is therefore important to incorporate into our own history the conflicts which that reality entails.

We meet tensions in all our relationships, even the deepest and most tender. For instance, love itself contains a dimension of desire and aggressiveness which can harm the other. Loving someone, in fact, means desiring a response from that person; it means entering that person's life, and such an intrusion leads to tensions. Accepting the nearness of another means taking the risk of sometimes hurting him or her and of being hurt.

The psychological history of individuals is also dotted with internal conflicts, feelings of guilt, private shame, and other crushing feelings. These tensions are often the result of interaction with others. Guilt feelings, for example, result from the internalization of parental or societal commands. In our history of relationships, forgiveness always has a place, whether it is directed toward parents, educators or other persons because of whom we suffer psychologically.

Other tensions go beyond individuals; these are the conflicts of interest which are due to the way society is organized. A workers' demonstration, for example, expresses the confrontation of opposing interests. Oppositions of this type are often experienced as aggressions. Nevertheless, they are not directly related with people's individual desires but find their roots in socioeconomic structures. Self-employed people, for instance, may feel personally overwhelmed by the claims of wage earners, while the latter feel that the former want a society in which they, the wage earners, are exploited. The outcome is, inevitably, conflicts which harm individuals but are beyond their intentions and power.

Besides these tensions linked to particular social structures, others spring simply from the "rational" organization of society. In the name of reason, morality, science and technology, a certain social violence is caused—probably with some reason! People are subjected to the demands of the technological organization of a complex society and to the ethical constraints necessary for communal living. But often the demands of rationality, the gigantism of technology, and the complexity of new standards overwhelm some people, and in a way harm everyone.

Whether related to internalized feelings, to interpersonal relationships, social structures or technologies, all conflicts involve hurt. Everybody feels their effects and carries the scars. All these sufferings are part of the human condition. They cause many individuals to isolate themselves with their wounds and to hide the contradictions which they live. In order to approach and "tame" all this, it is necessary to live forgiveness and to celebrate it.

Transgressions

Catholic moralists have taken more trouble to describe

standards and a supposedly ideal order than transgressions, i.e., the paths which lead individuals and groups to cross over the frontiers inside which cultural, ethical or religious traditions tend to confine them. And yet transgressions form part of life.

Everyone is born and is educated in a family, social class and culture which impose their own moral standards and methods of organizing life. These structures provide reassurance and indicate with some accuracy what one can expect of the world in which one lives. However, they are also a problem for individuals. Beyond the frontiers of what is permitted by these standards, people find it difficult to find their way. The space inside these standards, however, is often too narrow.

One day or another, the circumstances of life lead people to consider those limits critically and to consider overstepping them. The process begins with a feeling that certain aspects of the established order are intolerable. This feeling is generally confused and badly articulated. It reveals that the proposed standards no longer make it possible to live. It is more often expressed as a cry than as a word. It is, for example, what certain couples have felt in the face of the rules concerning contraception; or it is what is felt by many concerning an economic order in which the privileged are ever more privileged and the poor ever more oppressed and exploited. Furthermore, it is what has been felt in the past by scientists who were called upon to deny, in the name of their faith, what seemed to them to be virtually obvious, such as evolution or the age of the earth. Practically all human beings have felt themselves at times to be in an imposed and intolerable straitjacket; they have felt it impossible to live according to the framework of what was perceived as the norm.

Just as the crayfish must abandon its old body in order to grow, so is it sometimes necessary to slough off attitudes, beliefs and habits in order to go on living. This does not happen painlessly, for often what paralyzes now was formerly a source of life. This has been felt by many people brought up according to a puritan morality with respect to emotional life. The whole of their personality was being structured by this ethic when they discovered that it was stifling them.

Perhaps an existence is not yet adult if it has never yet ignored boundaries, or overstepped frontiers. These transitions may occur quietly as in those who gently but firmly move out of the grasp of overauthoritarian parents, or they may take place violently and painfully, as in the case of those who totally reject their families, religion, social class and morality in order to acquire their own voice. In any case, all individuals must, sometime or other, have their own say, live their own lives, assume their own responsibilities, and leave the status of minor in which they have lived a part of their existence. For some, the break is radical; for others it takes place gradually and imperceptibly.

The occasions for breaking with a submissive past are numerous. Many experience their first serious opposition to their parents as a transgression; for others, a new horizon will be opened up by participation in a protest march, a strike, or a sociopolitical movement. The first word of love or the first kiss may also reveal a previously forbidden world; again, there is the moment when one dares to admit to oneself that one no longer believes in certain religious concepts held during childhood. Jesus too committed transgressions. The first two chapters of Mark's gospel relate several of them: speaking with authority, casting out demons, healing lepers, forgiving sinners, associating with publicans and sinners, neglecting to fast, ignoring the sabbath, proclaiming persons to be more important than the law, etc. In this process he too moved out of the family orbit.

It is a fact of life: Saying "no" to rules and committing transgressions are part of the human condition. Confronted with them, human beings sometimes feel fear, fascination and hesitation; they sometimes enjoy them but in any case they live with them, blossom out or are wounded by them.

The dynamic of transgressions

The "transgression" I speak of here does not concern

actions contrary to the rules which one commits through weakness, as in the case of a youth who, having gotten drunk, goes against his sexual morality and is afterwards overcome with remorse. Such a youth does not transgress in the strict sense of the word; he only confirms the rule. Quite different, however, is an action whereby one decides deliberately to go ahead, knowing that things will not be the same afterwards. For example, when someone who has been brought up as a Catholic and has never missed Sunday Mass, decides in cold blood (though doubtless with powerful and mixed emotions) not to attend Mass, we can speak of transgression in the strict sense of the word; in making this gesture, the person concerned does not know what will change in him (or her) nor whither it will lead. In this sense, the transgression is an action which alters someone's position, which changes his or her social relationships and creates new ones. Let us look at another example: A person belonging to the middle class who attends a workers' demonstration or a civil rights rally, or a peace protest march, emerges from it changed. The experience alters that person's social relations. It was the same when some priests decided for the first time to change the forms of the liturgy. In each of these cases, a certain progression of ideas, certain hesitations and internal tensions generally precede the act and the changes coming as a result. In particular, what matters most in transgressions are the choices related to certain loyalties or to certain social or physical arrangements. At first sight some of these choices can appear minor, but their impact can often be much greater than the impact of a particular action which directly transgresses a rule.

The dynamic of transgressions begins with a cry which resounds deep down in the person and says that it is time to change. Cries and feelings precede words and reasoning. Then, in the face of the rules which are beginning to be challenged, comes reflection. This, however, can find a meaning only within the limits of the person's system of rules, reasons, and rationality. This system stems from the past history of the person, before the transgression. One cannot foresee what would—or will—happen when one decides to go ahead and transgress.

The step of transgression—and this is often what irritates certain moralists who are defenders of the established order—is therefore always irrational or, at least, a-rational. If we could know rationally what the outcome of the action we are planning would be, it would not be a transgression in the strict sense: No frontier would be crossed. As long as we can give a reason for our action, we are always within the rule. A transgression, on the other hand, is a step into the unknown where the rules no longer operate. That is why transgressions cannot be categorized by morality; we cannot say that they are either permitted or forbidden. But they are lived and they form part of human and Christian experience. They are rooted in that dimension of human life which cannot be enclosed in the overly narrow structures of reason, science, morality or even religion.

Yet, transgressions are not just gratuitous acts; they aim at other manners of being and other social relationships which are guessed at and hoped for in the name of an ideal which is at least implicit. They are not purely destructuring; they destroy a certain cultural and social order in order to create a new one. The latter is not entirely foreseeable but we transgress because we hope for some ideal in a more or less confused manner. We see it clearly, for example, in the case of strikes or popular demonstrations.

Transgression is generally preceded by an interior and sometimes unconscious progression. Sometimes reflection will have anticipated this destination toward which a person goes. In some cases, however, the old order is so rigid that it is difficult to imagine the outcome of the transgression. For instance, when a shy boy (or girl) finally dares to kiss a girl (or boy), this action may have been preceded by long reflection but may also have been an apparently more spontaneous impulse.

Transgressions, finally, are *violence*. They are reactions against another violence, that which is institutionalized in rules and social order (disorder). The two types of violence are present in existence. Institutionalized violence sometimes leads to deadlock and an intolerable situation; a transgression breaks the deadlock by the novelty which it introduces. However, even if they are liberating for some, transgressions often cause wounds; these form part of what will have to be celebrated in the feast of forgiveness asked and granted.

Sin

Up to now, we have examined tensions, conflicts and violence between human beings but have not mentioned the concept of sin.

A first dimension of sin is symbolized by the doctrine of original sin. This doctrine speaks of human society in which the mystery of evil is experienced in a history of exploitation, oppression and trampling of all kinds, leaving human beings murdered, wounded, plunged into a community of "non-love," and always to some extent accomplices in these evils. The mystery of evil penetrates the whole of existence and all of us share in it.

Another dimension of sin is linked to our situation and to our actions in our own history. Certain actions and attitudes are more directly part of the mystery of evil revealed in the history of salvation; we refer to these actions and attitudes as "sin." This history which speaks of the murder of Abel, of the oppression of the Hebrews, of the plan to have Uriah killed so that David could possess Bethsheba concerns God who "hears the cries of the people." This history continues today: Men and women—individually and collectively—do evil, and God is not indifferent to it.

a. The cries of the oppressed. Not everybody perceives the mystery of evil in the same way. For instance, those who organize society generally regard it as fairly well structured; after all, it is theirs. As shown in the parable of Lazarus and the rich man—whom the bible does not label as "bad"—it is difficult for the rich and powerful to hear what others would like to make known to them. They have difficulty in analyzing their contradictions. There we see an important difference between persons: Some know where their contradictions and ambiguities are, while others, often of good faith, are in ignorance. The parable of the publican and the Pharisee is interesting from this point of view. Is not the difference between them that one is able to perceive the contradictions of his life and the other not? For the rich and the powerful it is difficult to see their own ambiguities and therefore to "confess their sin." The poor and the dropouts see it more easily, because they are literally overwhelmed by their contradictions and difficulties.

The beginnings of awareness always start with a cry: that of the oppressed, the exploited, the widows, the orphans, who experience the mystery of evil. Sometimes it is a cry of hate; the oppressed hates the one who tramples him down. The oppressor sometimes realizes his situation through finding himself the object of hate. For example, a white person may start to think about racism on the day when he sees a black person's look of hatred; a priest or nun may be prompted to discover the practical contradictions of the religious life when they find themselves hated by those to whom they are devoting themselves.

The cries of the oppressed are generally full of anger and suffering, like those of black people affected by apartheid in South Africa, or those of some wings of the feminist movement. The contradictions of existence are revealed through the intrusion of these harsh voices. Cries of this nature may be criticized because they are not sufficiently rational, but the important thing is that someone should begin to speak and to reveal situations which henceforth will be described as evil. It is normal, moreover, for the cries of the oppressed to be generally badly articulated and even incoherent. The word is, in fact, already a social power; those without power manage only with difficulty to put forward a word which will fit in with the arguments of those who organize society. That is why it is hardly reasonable to blame the oppressed for not having the coherence of university lecturers: If they had it, with all the social power which it implies, they would not be oppressed.

b. Prophetic voices. If we confined ourselves to these cries, the awareness of new sins would not be possible. It is still necessary to have the help of prophetic voices which can strongly articulate a first sympathetic understanding of aspirations which are as yet confused. Prophets say in words what is screamed out in cries; furthermore, by symbolic transgressions they restructure the social field. Thus, Jeremiah took a pot and broke it. Hosea behaved in an unexpected way to his unfaithful wife. In this way, both these persons caused people to move away from their normal routines. Prophetic acts and voices do not fall within the usual categories of the prevailing culture, of science, reason and established morality.

The prophets give legitimacy to a renewal; in denouncing injustices unrecognized up to that time, they give a new name to sin. Their word differs from that of those who "appropriate" the cries of the oppressed. "False prophets" endeavor to incorporate protests into the order of reason, science and morality, so that in the end the cries lose all social impact. Prophecy itself is not designed to win over dissenting opinion. It says more or less the following to the people: "You are concerned over rules which you find very important. You consider that this or that type of sacrifice is pleasing to God. You have a morality and you believe that, if you follow it, God is satisfied. Well, be aware that Yahweh hardly cares at all about your little sins, those you cherish through your examinations of conscience. But in the midst of the people there is a new sin, which has not yet been called by that name. This sin has been revealed by the cries of the oppressed people and Yahweh is listening to his people's cry." In this way, the prophet points out something new in a precise historical situation.

c. New ethical arguments. At the start, people, particularly those on the spot, consider the prophet is insane. Then, some begin to find that he or she is partly right. A new ethical argument begins to be worked out which will take account of what is revealed. In time, the new way of seeing things is generally more and more accepted, so that it is included in textbooks of morals and thus takes its place in the ethical heritage of a society. It becomes part of the moral law which structures people and groups.

The process of becoming aware of a new sin in a community may be short or long. Awareness in the United

States that slavery could be termed "sin" was slow. There was a period when plantation owners possessed their slaves without feeling guilty about it. The cries of the exploited went completely unheard in that society. Owners could not imagine the *reason* for certain revolts and hatreds. The Quakers started very soon to articulate these cries; there came a point when they were no longer able to reconcile slavery with the gospel. But it was several centuries more before the majority finally felt that slavery was immoral and therefore a sin which had to be described as such.

This collective process has its equivalent in interpersonal relations. A process of reflection which will lead to a request for forgiveness often begins, for example, because of the tears of the loved and wounded being. There, too, suffering is the beginning of thought and awareness.

This historical vision of sin confronts individuals with an important question: Are they the first or the last to perceive what a society begins to see as unacceptable? For instance, while the Quakers were already protesting against slavery in the 17th century, religious congregations continued to practice it until it was abolished. For a whole series of reasons which deserve to be analyzed in depth, they had never heard the prophetic voices. Like the brothers of the rich man in the parable of the poor Lazarus, these congregations—probably because of their choice of loyalties—found themselves unable to see what raised problems and were unable to listen to the prophets.

A historical concept of sins

Some people regard sins in the way animal species used to be regarded before the theory of evolution: They imagine them to be fixed once and for all. In point of fact, the Bible does not furnish a fixed list of sins which is linked to a non-temporal order. Sins, processes of awareness, requests for forgiveness, and conversions are historical realities. The living word of God speaks through the prophets of God and helps God's people to become converted continually and to ask for forgiveness. From this viewpoint, the discovery of a new type of sin (for example, sexism) should not be perceived as crushing but rather as positive. Indeed, to discern a new sin is also to perceive that the Spirit, at work among us, brings us liberation. The discovery of a new sin should therefore be celebrated as a fresh manifestation of God, and not experienced as a crushing burden on consciences.

This discovery of sin can take place healthily only if accompanied by great tenderness. For those who do not feel themselves unconditionally accepted, the awareness of unsuspected contradictions is extremely threatening. On the contrary, we can rejoice at discovering a new sin when we live this new awareness in the peace and joy of those who know they are loved. No one can live solely in the harshness of conflicts, increasing awareness and transgressions. Another dimension is also needed, a dimension of encounter between those who live relationships which are social, sometimes pleasant, sometimes painful, and often full of conflict. The first step in this encounter is a request: a request for forgiveness, a request which does not abolish the harshness of the conflicts, which does not necessarily lead to a reconciliation but which refuses to reduce social relationships to their conflicts.

Forgiveness

When one becomes aware of the clashes of interpersonal and societal life, a question often looms on the horizon and is addressed to others: "Do you accept me as I am, amid all the tensions which we live?" This is a request for acceptance, despite all the limitations present. Such a request goes against both isolation and violence. Isolation is a temptation which is often felt in the face of experienced limitations. Violence, imposed on others, is a temptation in the opposite direction. On the other hand, the request is an opening to a certain vulnerability; it is a form of relationship implying trust. Trust is not always easy in groups which live under the sway of business, or competition, or justification by works; in such circles, one is not sufficiently at ease to ask, for nothing is free and most people live in the isolation of a protective shell. The request for forgiveness implies and causes an opening in the armor in which isolated persons enclose themselves. What characterizes the request is the resolution not to reduce others, especially adversaries, to the picture one forms of them during the conflict; it is also the persistence of the desire to meet them, despite the enmity or the clashes which separate. But these attitudes do not abolish conflicts and struggles; sometimes, moreover, they must be restrained in order to ensure that they are not perverted and absorbed into a false harmony which erases the differences. The request for forgiveness in no way means allowing oneself to be captured by the dream of a unity which hopes for acceptance by all and for a life without struggle.

It is all this that Christian traditions invite us to celebrate in the sacrament of forgiveness: tensions, conflicts, transgressions, prophetic words or actions, the confession of new sins, the request for forgiveness, and the acceptance of the forgiveness accorded.

Although forgiveness is a dimension of all relational life, it is lived especially at precise moments and on particular points, for example, when prophetic voices or special events make us more aware of a particular contradiction in life; living forgiveness then assumes a special meaning. In our day, for example, many perceive that men-women relationships are structured by "sexism," i.e., that situation in which men dominate while women adopt an attitude of submission. For this reason, people wish today to ask forgiveness for sexism. Not that sexism is anything very new; what is new is our awareness, which therefore brings with it a fresh request for forgiveness.

What is a sin?

We shall therefore define sin on the basis of forgiveness: Sin is that for which we wish to ask forgiveness and which has been revealed to us by the cry of the oppressed and/or by the voices of the prophets.

An interesting point about this definition is that it does not link sin and culpability. After all, in order to request forgiveness of someone for something, it is not necessary to be in the wrong. Any relationship involves wounds for which one may wish to request forgiveness, without being aware of wrong in this any more than in anything else. For example, membership in a white Western society living partly on the exploitation of the third world may cause us to wish to ask forgiveness of the people we are exploiting; while there is not much point in feeling individually guilty, there is point in asking forgiveness. The same thing applies in interpersonal relations. In a friendship, for example, I may hurt the other person while pursuing a positive end which I do not regret. I can then request forgiveness for the harm done, without regretting my line of action. More illuminating still on this point is the situation of teachers and parents; in the educational process, they find themselves inflicting hurt for which they will ask forgiveness, but without feeling guilty on that account.

Following the same argument, concepts of *sin* and of *request for forgiveness* are not automatically linked to the concept of regret. A certain type of regret is, of course, always valid; unless one is a sadist, one would prefer not to have harmed the other party. However, this does not necessarily imply regret for what one has done, because it is impossible to live in a relationship without sometimes inflicting hurt. Often, moreover, those who imagine they can refrain from clashing with others do it just the same, particularly by the way in which they skirt around conflicts.

As soon as one lives with others, one sometimes hurts them. That is what is shown by Christian traditions, which remind us that we are all sinners. Recognition of the inevitable dimension of evil leads us to terminate the tiring and painful game of counting and measuring everything. One of the freeing messages of the gospel is precisely the proclamation that God does not measure and that we are unconditionally loved. It is therefore not necessary always to know whether one has behaved well or badly. This liberation does not bring with it indifference to the wounds that one inflicts; instead, it opens the way to the system of relationships belonging specifically to the kingdom of God: Everyone is forgiven and, consequently, can live in the tenderness of those who cease to measure themselves constantly. Moreover, when a person feels most unconditionally accepted and loved, what is most positive in him or her is revealed.

Most people, however, are incapable of bearing the social risk connected with a God who loves without conditions. What will happen, they think, if God does not gauge or measure? Accordingly, they replace the evangelical concept of unconditional forgiveness by a concept of sin which ultimately serves either for social control and support of the established order, or for their liberation struggles. Forgiveness, on the contrary, is an attitude which prevents a point of view from becoming absolute and which can thereby help to reject all totalitarianisms, whether of the right or of the left.

The celebration of forgiveness

a. The discovery of sins. The sacrament of penance or forgiveness is rooted in the unconditional love of God in the midst of our contradictions. It is therefore important that this unconditional love be proclaimed at the very center of the celebration. This sacrament is not primarily a means of being "better" but rather the celebration of forgiveness. It celebrates the fact that conflicts, tensions, transgressions and clashes between human beings are exactly the situations that call forth our hope; God is present in the middle of these realities. That is why the discovery of the contradictions in a Christian community should not be overwhelming; this community may express in its celebrations the joy of discovering new types of sins. When, through prophetic voices, it begins to perceive a new way in which the liberation of God is at work, this deserves celebration. The discovery of new sins is very different from the conventional examinations of conscience; the prophetic dimension of these examinations was often small. The discovery of new sins, however, opens up horizons. This was the case when the Christians began to struggle against slavery or when they refused to recognize that owners had almost unlimited rights over means of production; or, today, when some people find that our society treats women as inferiors and call that "sin." Naming new sins in this way during celebrations does not radically transform the situations but it does cause a process of change. The same applies when Christians change their attitudes toward the investment of their money and begin to wonder whether it is not being used to exploit populations. This is a "new sin" which is pointed out by prophetic voices. It is important to celebrate this new awareness and the hope linked to it. In this way a conversion process goes on, that is, a change of mentality and attitude; it enables Christians to share in the work of liberation which comes from God and operates in history.

b. Celebrating hope and its signs. Besides the discovery of "new sins," the signs of hope represented by victories of freedom and partial reconciliations must be celebrated; at those moments something resembling the peace of the kingdom appears. Of course, there is never any total reconciliation on earth. Injustice is always present, so that Christian traditions speak of total reconciliation only from an eschatological viewpoint, in the fullness of time. Even in the happiest relationships and in the most harmonious groups, limitations are discovered. There are fortunately moments at which the agreement attained is already felt: times of reconciliation in homes, nations, or between different social groups. At such moments, new social relationships seem to foreshadow what otherwise can as yet be lived only in hope. This is the case, for example, when enterprises succeed in achieving a degree of self-management; even if this does not last very long, such events show life on the march. These "transgressions" of established routines point the way to the possibility of establishing new social relationships less marked by the usual oppression and exploitation. These successes are to be celebrated even if they still have their limitations. In fact, one of the qualities of the poor and oppressed is to know how to celebrate without waiting for all problems to be solved, without waiting for justice to be established on earth. They know that if they were to await the coming of justice, they would never celebrate. The slogan "no celebration without justice" corresponds to the unhappy conscience of the rich and powerful.

In the sacrament of forgiveness, therefore, all the

powerful reconciliations and liberations of history are celebrated, whether it is the liberation of a nation after the departure of a dictator, the reunion of a crisis-struck family, a successful strike, the deliverance of the Hebrew people from Egypt, the renewal of the alliance between Yahweh and his people, etc. All these events evoke hope for a total liberation and reconciliation symbolized in the new alliance of the Last Supper. Hoping for this is essential if, in the midst of the struggles of today, we are to celebrate the opening to new life, which is symbolized by resurrection.

c. Sacrament of forgiveness or sacrament of reconciliation? To live forgiveness is surely to hope for reconciliation, but it is not yet necessarily to experience that reconciliation. It may still remain a very distant or even utopian prospect. Forgiving and receiving forgiveness in the middle of a conflict leads partners or opponents (individual or collective) to recognize each other in their differences and even their opposition, without reducing each other to these oppositions; it is also to go beyond the negation of others and the isolation of oneself often generated by conflicts.

For example, a couple may live forgiveness while knowing that they will still have to resolve their differences and without denying that they remain opposed; exploited persons may forgive their exploiters, while struggling hard for their rights. Forgiveness thus opens up a new human dimension and even a tenderness in conflicts without abolishing them. But to try to use forgiveness as a way of denying the conflict would be a perversion. To be able to speak of *reconciliation,* injustices must have ceased and, as far as possible, some reparation made. Too often the sacrament of forgiveness is perverted by making it into a way of denying the reality of conflict and confusing forgiveness and reconciliation. That is why the expression "sacrament of reconciliation" is ambiguous, for while the sacrament speaks of a hope and promise of reconciliation, it always remains only partially fulfilled.

d. Asking forgiveness. At the root of the celebration is the request for forgiveness. To know how to *ask* is important in life. Nothing, in fact, is more painful than to close oneself up without daring to ask for anything. It is perhaps difficult and sometimes impossible to address the request to the persons or groups directly concerned; but the expression of the request, if only ritual, nonetheless has a meaning. That is the meaning of the "confession of sins." Tradition is not content with a simple and purely inward confession addressed directly to God. It proposes a ritual of request for forgiveness and of avowal of sins designed to draw a person out from isolation and into touch with what is lived. This request is not lived solely by the individual but has a community dimension. Confession is not intended to be painful and to produce sensations of guilt; this would be a perversion. The practice of the ritual word of request for forgiveness, however, possesses a human force which is much greater than simple internal prayer.

For a healthy celebration of the confession of sins, a process of "liberating listening" is necessary. This is a service which the community should make available, especially through some of its ministers: to listen to the request for forgiveness and in this way to enable each of the individuals and groups to say how they are living human relationships and how they hope to be accepted and loved. The ministry of listening is not always easy in a society which measures everything and which is thereby guilt-producing. To know how to listen, like Jesus, without producing guilt is unfortunately an attitude that is much too rare in the church and her ministers.

e. The expression of forgiveness. Finally, it is necessary to proclaim in the community that forgiveness is given, and given completely; the celebration must affirm that God and, as far as possible, the Christian community, accept persons unconditionally. Over and beyond social conflicts and relational tensions, tenderness must be shared. Christians must say to one another, "I accept you as you are." Forgiving in this way does not mean granting mercy or pity from the heights of one's condescension; nor does it necessarily mean approval. What it does mean is unconditional recognition of the other or others, while remaining aware of their limitations and even of the conflicts in which they may continue to oppose us. This total acceptance is a gracious gift of God to human beings. However, it will not be manifested if we do not express it to one another; it is therefore the responsibility of all human beings to make acceptance visible and audible to one another.

It may also be particularly important that someone would be able sometimes to express forgiveness not only in his or her own name but also in the name of the whole Christian community, in the name of the church. It is the traditional role of the priest to be qualified to make God's forgiveness manifest by proclaiming it on behalf of the whole Christian community. In this sense, absolution completes the celebration of forgiveness, insofar as it is absolution which publicly expresses the gift and unconditional forgiveness of God. Through absolution, the priest, who is the spokesperson of the church, accepts into the eucharistic community whoever so requests, thereby making known the acceptance of God.

Finally, this sacrament must be lived in great tenderness, even if conflicts persist. This tenderness is the experience of those who know that they are forgiven all and who yet share the paralysis of human sin. It is the tenderness of those who say: "We are all guilty, we are all involved in conflicts, we have all been wounded, we are still being wounded; that it why it is no longer worthwhile counting. Like companions receiving God's love freely, let us live forgiveness in goodness with one another, with the tenderness of those who have experienced too many sufferings together to wish to add to them." This kind of tenderness liberates, provided, however, that it does not merge into a fusion of harmony that erases differences; it can be celebrated in joy, even if we know that the conflicts are not yet resolved nor the wounds healed.

"Penance"

For many centuries, the celebration of forgiveness has traditionally ended in a request by the priest, on behalf of the Christian community, for a symbolic act sometimes known as "penance." This act is sometimes perceived as "reparation" or "attempted reparation." Such an interpretation is valid but is liable to refer back to a universe of exchange, measurement, and justification by works, from which the gospel tends, in fact, to lead us away. It overlooks the fact that forgiveness is free; it may even lead to the confusion of Christian forgiveness with the typical "fair exchange" reflex of our societies. In the Christian community, one is not forgiven because one is capable of making reparation. On the contrary, it is important to learn to receive without feeling any need to give in return.

Furthermore, there is meaning in expressing by a symbolic gesture the coming to life of a community aware of the liberating action of God in its midst. From this point of view, it can be understood that the community, through its presiding officer, may designate a symbolic action which will render the struggle for justice and the action of God in history more real to everyone. In addition, the call to reparation may symbolically mark the distance between the forgiveness lived today and a reconciliation which is still always partial.

7 | Marriage: Celebration of Love in Relationships

In our culture, the first thing that marriage celebrates is encounter, love and the hope of a new home. Generally, this is fairly easily marked: The bride and bridegroom choose texts which express how they see themselves as a couple and how they wish to build a family. In the best situations this choice is made with others, parents and/or friends. The celebration expresses their hope, tenderness, joy, mutual respect, and differences, but also their fears. The witnesses are able to say how they have observed the couple's growth in love and its effect on others.

It is also necessary to celebrate the hope represented for society by the establishment of a family; this is an opening to the future. It is not easy to trust the future to the point of bringing children into the world. Marriage is the celebration of the continuance of life in the face of all that threatens it.

A celebration of marriage, however, does not only express the commitment of two human beings to each other and the establishment of a family; it is also a celebration through which a community senses its network of relationships and the way in which these relationships can be either liberating or oppressive. Beyond good wishes for the couple, who imagine that they are going to change the world, the celebration must summon up all the tensions connected with the family, those which relate to the new spouses and those which accompany the restructuring of

117

relationships that follow marriage. It is important, for example, that the celebration should not exclude those feelings of separation experienced by the parents of the newlyweds on seeing their children begin a home. Thus, depending on the particular circumstances, different feelings will be celebrated. In any case marriage celebrates more than what is experienced by a couple isolated from the rest of society: Like the other sacraments, it is a celebration of the whole church which, in the structures of marriage, lives the hope of the kingdom. It is necessary therefore to place the marriage of Christians in both a historical context and in the context of society. We must also see it as the gift of God.

Marriage as a social institution, and its ambiguities

In every society, there exists an institution corresponding more or less to what we call "marriage." This institution ensures that children are brought up and that parents enjoy enough security at the time when they are indispensable to the children. It is necessary in view of human biology, since a certain period of time is needed for a human being to be able to manage alone. That is why, in all cultures, marriage is geared more to the children than to the couple. In fact, a view of marriage centered on love and on the couple is rare, and is a characteristic of our modern society which caters to the individual and the private. Only recently has stress been placed, in our industrialized society, on the "second end of marriage," namely, the self-realization of the couple.

All societies have a family system, but not all accept the existence of families, if by these we mean the family group to which we are accustomed: father, mother and children. What is found everywhere is a societal organization revolving around children and the bonds of kinship. Depending on the society, there exist different family systems characterized by more or less well-defined social roles. These systems structure relationships and alliances whose economic, political and emotional dimensions determine who the "kin" are. The new links that result may be exalting and freeing, but they are not without ambivalence. In fact, by creating some social links, marriage breaks or at least loosens others. Parents will thus cease to see their married child as often as before; the child will henceforth lead an independent life. These changes do not occur painlessly, as the numerous difficulties experienced with in-laws prove. Friends of the married couple also feel the difference, because home life leads the new spouses to rearrange their ties of friendship.

Furthermore, new economic considerations are linked to marriage; so true is this that insurance companies do not always apply the same conditions to married as to unmarried people. In some cases, one of the partners (in our culture, usually the woman) gives up dwelling place, previous contacts, and even name.

The relationships thus created are not without ambiguity or even without injustice. While it provides a useful and beneficial organization, marriage also generates social controls and sometimes oppression. In some cultures, it is even difficult to free oneself from the family grip; men and women forever belong to their tribe and family. In the West, the family system bears the weight of a sexist patriarchal culture.

One can appreciate in this context the cultural impact of the words of scripture telling those who marry to leave their parents, as also the importance of Jesus' decision to put a gap between himself and his family clan and to assert that his family consists of all those who listen to God's word.

As it is easier to express the joy of love than the tensions linked to family systems, it may be useful to consider the development of the family in the West; it will help to situate marriage and family in their social context.

Western family institutions

The patriarchal family was characterized in the Middle Ages by an extended group generally living in self-sustained economy. On the whole, this group was able to look after itself; it was composed of grandparents, children, uncles and aunts, servants and also domestic animals such as cows, pigs, and particularly cats and dogs. The family basically was structured by the land itself, as farmers know even today. Since then, primarily for economic reasons (connected with the rise of the bourgeois and then industrial society), a new type of family has appeared on the scene: the nuclear family (made up of parents and children). This pattern seems to have already been the rule in England in the 15th century. But for a long time afterwards, servants continued to form part of the family group, with non-verbal customary contracts: A family had responsibilities toward all its members including domestics, i.e., all those who lived in the *domus,* the house. It is only in an already highly advanced industrial society that the master of the house considered himself to have the right to dismiss a servant who was no longer needed.

In the 15th and 16th centuries the family took its structure more from the couple than from the enlarged group. In the 20th century the movement is accelerating; uncles and aunts are less and less regarded as members of the family group. The dwelling place is generally separated from the place of work; the home has become an apartment where the couple live with their children, isolated from the rest of society (although linked to the world by the telephone and television). Local mobility has altered the ties of a family whose members may sometimes live thousands of miles away from one another. Thus has been born the "private family" made up of the parents and, for a few years, of the children. After they have reached their adolescence most offspring cease to spend their holidays with their parents; the latter are usually alone after the age of 50. At the same time, the happiness of the couple becomes increasingly more important; more and more people marry for love and fewer and fewer for economic, political or social reasons.

For the family these changes lead to the loss of some of its social roles. It no longer performs a social security role, while less than a century ago, when someone was sick, old or unemployed, that person's needs were met by the relatives. The family's educational role has also diminished: The school, attendance at which is now compulsory, has taken over. The transition emerges clearly when the role of the family in sex education is considered. Some people think that this is the parents' job alone, while other believe that most of today's parents are incapable of tackling the task. The extended family was undoubtedly more fitted to fulfil it than the isolated couple. Even if certain burdens have been removed from the family, however, the parents find themselves with enormous responsibilities which weigh upon them more heavily than in the past. It is often the couple alone—and sometimes one single parent—who must bear the burden of giving the children economic and emotional security. If husband and wife got on badly before, the extended family could fill the gap: The children had many adults who formed a stable environment around them. Young people in our post-industrial society, however, have only one certainty, and even that is not entirely secure, the certainty that when their parents move, they will take their children with them. But the children cannot be really sure about the rest of their surroundings; their family has been reduced to little more than a consumer unit.

How celebrate the social dimension of marriage?

Trusting the future, along with hope and love, does not come automatically. It is necessary therefore to express in the rite the tensions and ambiguities of the family system in our society. Thus, while avoiding the mistake of moralizing, a true celebration would bring out the type of relationship which governs our industrial system, in which people have scarcely any knowledge of, or contact with, one another. It would speak of the tension caused by a mobile society and by the aspiration to find roots. It would recall the heavy burden on the couple, who, with respect to the children, must work without the safety net of the extended family. It would also recall the relations between the nuclear family and the school or other broader communities. It would bring out the pressures of the consumer society on the family system.

The description of these tensions cannot remain the product of an abstract sociological reflection; it must answer the questions of young people, who are explicitly or implicitly aware of the pressures which they are meeting and who know about the ambiguities and pitfalls of the family system. (That is why some even hesitate to get married.)

The celebration should avoid excessive emphasis on the couple and the nuclear family, even if this is the fashion in certain family movements.[1] Undoubtedly, the positive aspects of the couple's relationship and of the emotional life should be stressed, but it would be naive to think that such emphasis is nothing but beneficial to families. It is therefore important to look both benevolently and critically at celebrations which center exclusively on an ideology of love of the couple without perceiving all the ambiguity or even the threats which are hidden therein.

Contemporary insistence on the "psychological maturity necessary for the marriage commitment" (on pain of invalidity of the marriage!) is also not without ambiguity. What does being "mature enough" mean? There are no doubt links between this requirement of maturity, the isolation of the couple in society, and the many and various roles which are expected of it. The call for "maturity" is part of the ideological support system given to an overburdened family cultural pattern. It is a way to "moralize" and to preach to the couple.

Some reserve is also necessary with respect to those who believe that everything must in any case be solved by love. Practically, it amounts to formulating another moral standard (and burden, and sometimes guilt) to be imposed on the couple. The attributing of excessive importance to love is liable to be only one more way of hiding the conflicts

---

1. Actually, it is generally when an institution is in difficulty or overburdened that there is a tendency to emphasize it ideologically so that individuals will accept the heavy tasks which it proposes. For instance, the work ethic appeared at a time when, with the mercantile society and division of labor, people no longer saw clearly the results of their efforts. Likewise, some people consider that the tendency to overemphasize the couple and to create some "family spirituality" or family movements is the result of an overburdening of the institution. Because much is asked of it, it is given proportionately greater importance.

associated with the family and, more particularly, with the couple in the nuclear family.

Marriage as a sacrament

Marriage is therefore a social institution varying from one culture to another. Christians have recognized in it a sacred gift of God. For some, this means that an institution, "Christian marriage," exists which brings together the quintessence of all the positive elements of the various family systems. This often amounts to regarding as virtually sacred one institutional model of the family as the only one. Those who consider the sacrament of marriage in this way generally end, while defending what they call *the* marriage, by legitimizing the established order in their cultural context! In the view of others, however, human reality itself becomes the sacrament; the human institution in all its fullness is assumed by God and becomes the sign and the guarantee of God's gift represented by human love and the growth of the human race. In asserting the sacramentality of marriage, such Christians proclaim their hope that the very human social institution that is marriage can be the image of God's love for the people.

There are therefore two attitudes toward the origin of the sacramentality of marriage: those who see a direct divine institution in marriage, and those who consider the historical human institution itself as the site of God's gift. In the view of the latter, the reality of the sacrament is the real-life family experience itself, which is looked at as the sign of God's alliance with the people and of the fidelity of Christ and the church. This is the viewpoint which I adopt.

Sin and salvation in family institutions

Such a view takes seriously the human reality of marriage, and in it too, therefore, sees sin, a dimension nowadays too often absent or caricatured to such an extent that it sometimes becomes difficult during certain celebrations of the sacrament to discover any trace of the mystery of redemption.

There is no question here of wishing to reintroduce guilt-producing and unhealthy concepts of a certain family ethics from which the majority of Christians have fortunately freed themselves. Rather is it the intention to recognize the mystery of evil present in society and in family systems. An examination of the various family institutions shows their basic ambiguities; in theological terms, they could be analyzed through the notion of original sin. Family institutions are both the site of oppression and exploitation (whether one is talking of the place of women in many of them, systems of inheritance, the economic and political alliances involved therein, power games, etc.) and the site of hope (tenderness, forgiveness, liberation, love received and returned, the welcoming of future generations, etc.). To speak of the family without recognizing this ambivalence is to be rather naive and, in any case, to place oneself at a distance from most theologies of redemption. The powerful and liberating love of God is, indeed, at work precisely in this ambivalent world, this world of sin; that is what should be celebrated in the sacrament.

Too often, celebrations of marriage overlook the mystery of evil, considering over hastily that marriage is totally good in itself. Celebrations often resort, implicitly or explicitly, to a concept of the "nature" of the family as determined by God, or to an idyllic view of marriage. Historically, however, the family is a human, very human, and sometimes bloody institution, structured simultaneously out of sin and salvation. As Catholics, should we not acquire a somewhat greater awareness of the intuition of Luther on this point? Has not the insistence of many Catholic theologians on speaking of a nature "good in itself" sometimes led them to weaken the force of the mystery of redemption and the tension between the mystery of evil and the liberation of human beings? Would not a more precise analysis of the oppressions, alienations, exploitations, guilt sensations linked to family systems bring out the whole force of the hope which dares to see, through these human institutions, a sign of God's love for the people, a love which the scriptures present as a difficult relationship made up of tenderness, infidelity and forgiveness?

From this point of view, asserting that marriage is a

sacrament implies a hope which goes beyond individual or even interpersonal salvation; speaking of salvation must affect all human institutions and, first of all, the family system which is the basis of any society. The sacrament of marriage thus foreshadows the kingdom, although this mystery of salvation is absent from sacramental theologies which make little effort to integrate the dimensions of sin and forgiveness.

Such a point of view also restores the place of the various family institutions in different cultures; none is perfect but all are the site of salvation.[2] Such a sacramental theology makes it possible not to ask Christians of other cultures to first switch over to a certain cultural pattern before speaking of the sacramentality of marriage. It avoids the naive belief that the model of marriage produced in the West is a unique ideal to be imposed everywhere. On the contrary, from a stoutly Pauline viewpoint, it could be said that the Good News shows both sin and the gift of God in all these family systems.

Such a viewpoint of hope is particularly fitted to societies—like ours—undergoing change. Our contemporaries will thus understand the meaning in celebrating family institutions in which so much uncertainty prevails today as a site of the manifestation of the love of God and the growth of God's kingdom.

The question of fidelity

Insofar as marriage celebrates the commitment of persons, the celebration must speak of fidelity. In Christian traditions, human fidelity symbolizes that of God, who loves despite difficulties. Fidelity can therefore not be reduced to the prohibition of adultery and thus narrowed down to a purely physical and biological concept. A morality which is overly centered on sexuality sometimes overlooks the more general dimension of fidelity. This consists, in fact, in accepting in a responsible way all the

2. As a result of these ideas, a question may arise: Is it right that the church should continue to keep the sort of civil record which it assumed as a service in the Middle Ages? Should it not celebrate the gift of God in civil or common-law marriages?

bonds that one has created or that one has accepted through life's circumstances. In point of fact, concrete fidelities will require a sharing between various competing and conflicting relationships and loyalties; this will bring tensions which must be reflected and explored in the celebration. Fidelity to the children will take time that cannot be spent with the spouse; fidelity between spouses will sometimes conflict with the bond which they have with their parents, their loyalty to their original family; at the time of engagement or marriage, the couple must also renegotiate the time and importance devoted to former friends; the spouses will have to find their place with respect to the various emotional relationships present in their life, as also with respect to the obligations of their profession and their commitment to social causes. Fidelity then ceases to appear as an abstract ideal or simply as the opposite of adultery; it is a dynamic quest for the compromises to be found between different and sometimes conflicting human bonds, none of which can be eliminated: bonds with spouses, children, parents, friends, members of the same social class or with workmates, professional relations, etc. These various human loyalties sometimes succeed in reaching an easy harmony; but there are many cases where the different links appear to be in conflict or even incompatible. At such times rather simplistic recipes are too short: It is necessary to find the compromises that seem best, or sometimes simply the least bad. All this underlies marriage, and a wedding celebration which does not take it into account is likely to lack deep human consistency. It must show that while marriage can convey economic, political and cultural oppressions, it can also be the site of tenderness and encounter, of openness, generosity, love received and given, intimacy overcoming isolation, and forgiveness. Faced with this mysterious ambiguity, Christian traditions, making a final wager on hope, have recognized marriage to be a sacrament.

Perversions of the sacrament of marriage

Nowadays some young—and sometimes not so

young—people are distrustful of marriage, particularly Catholic marriage. It strikes them as a trap rather than as the celebration of hope. The church's insistence upon the indissolubility of marriage seems to them to be a new form of social control whereby society forces people back into its order; marriage is one of the institutions through which young people "settle down."

In fact, the "trap" of the family system is present in nearly all societies. The gospel bears the mark of this trap; Jesus finds himself tackled one day by his family, who want to take him over again and bring him back into line. He then says certain words which, seen in their social context, are truly meaningful: "My mother and my brothers— they are those who hear the word of God"; he refuses to be the slave of the family system. From this viewpoint, the sacrament of marriage has to be a celebration of the hope of Christians and not a confirmation of the ambiguities of a family system.

Marriage as a trap is approached in a crucial manner when the question of divorce is raised. For Christians, marriage, the symbol of God's love for the people, can never be destroyed. Furthermore, any human relation is indissoluble. Simple friendship weaves bonds between people which can never be claimed not to have existed; one cannot return to indifference. All our relationships shape us, whether we have forged them ourselves or simply accepted them, or even whether they have been imposed on us. There is no sense in acting as if our relationships never existed; one cannot know how they will or should be lived in the future, but it is absurd to deny them. They could be truly said to be "indissoluble."

In this sense, the indissolubility of marriage is central to Christian traditions; marriage creates a deep human bond which will have to be accepted. However, accepting this bond in no way means that "staying together" is a solution to every marital crisis. Faithfulness to this bond must, like all fidelity, be negotiated in the midst of sometimes conflicting loyalties. There is nothing to prove that the most Christian compromise is not sometimes to divorce and contract another union (which the church will not recognize as a sacrament). To present Christian marriage as a sort of rigid program in which indissolubility is the one and only value so that all other values are evaded would simply be to make God the guardian of social control. That is what God obviously is not.

The Christian community must do everything to ensure that marriage is not seen as a trap. It must itself remain faithful to the couple, as God is faithful. When a marriage is in difficulty and departs from the usual standards, is it not deplorable when the Christian community sometimes crushes it further with its judgment and pressures? Adopting this attitude is a false witness to the fidelity of God, which accompanies human beings through all their travails, understanding rather than judging them.

The community is therefore called upon to bear witness to the fidelity of God, regardless of the couple's difficulties or deviations. It is important that this call should be expressed in celebration and that the community should say clearly that if the marriage becomes difficult, the community is with the couple on their journey, trying to be faithful to them as God is faithful. The community will in this way discover more deeply how this new home concerns them and how the success of human love depends greatly on the way in which the community acts toward the couple and the children. In this sense, Christian marriage must be a feast of the community which desires to be faithful to the newly married, not in order to crush, judge or control them but to be the sign of the fidelity of God to the people. The sacrament of marriage is in this way called upon to celebrate the love—the gracious gift of God—which is lived in the family and in the whole network of human relationships.

8 | Orders: Confronting and Celebrating the Question of Power

Regarding the sacrament of ordination, I shall adopt a point of view close to the one I employed in speaking of the institution and sacrament of marriage. In that case, I held that, faced with an institution related to economic, political and cultural dimensions, and therefore linked to ambiguous interests, the gospel tradition placed stress on a hope, the hope that, through all this, another reality may be lived which will ultimately be revealed as a gift of God. In the same way, the sacrament of ordination shows that, through the realities of power, Christian communities hope to meet a God who liberates, rather than people who oppress and exploit. This hope does not, of course, abolish the ambiguities expressed by the doctrine of original sin; it is not easy, it is even impossible, to exercise power in a completely liberating manner. The problem is therefore to see how the institutions of power—the established orders—can be lived in the most evangelical manner possible.

Ordination is the celebration of the institutionalization of power in the Christian community. It is a first step which decreases the arbitrary, for the institution provides for the giving of a mandate which will protect the community against those who otherwise would impose their will. It is a protection, especially for the weak and oppressed, but it can also bring about abuses.

The problem of power in a group

For many Christians, the clergy are a problem. Some see an abuse of clerical power; others, a lack of leadership. Christians often react to clericalism by proposing remedies for correcting and eliminating it. I would propose the opposite approach. After all, the problem of power is fundamental in any human community and there is nothing to suggest that things will be much better in another system tomorrow. The important thing is perhaps not to eliminate the problem introduced by power and leadership, but to succeed in living it in as positive a way as possible. My argument is that, if a sacrament of ordination exists and if there are rights that relate to the transmission of powers in the church, it is precisely because power always involves tension or crises in communities. That is probably why all societies have rites linked to power and its transmission. The sacrament of ordination appears then to be only a special case of a ritualization which is found virtually everywhere. Just as all groups have a feast of birth, initiation to adulthood or full membership, or marriage, so also have they rituals related to the difficulties arising from the exercise of power. To master this difficult reality there is nothing better than rites.

In a group, there are always tensions, if only because of the varying desires of the persons composing the group. Furthermore, as soon as a group is in any way organized, different interests come to the fore. These originate not only in individual personalities but also and simply from the different positions occupied in the social organization. For instance, in a class, the teacher's interest does not coincide with the interests of the students, simply because of their different situations in the scholastic institution. In practically all groups, the relationship of each member to power or to the organization introduces some associations of oppression. The same applies to the social images conveyed by a culture; sexism, for example, is an ideology which allows relationships between men and women to be transformed quickly into oppressive situations. This is also the case when the distinction between clergy and laity brings with it the practical negation of the contribution of each person to the community.

The institution of power

Power conflicts are inevitable; that is why all societies institutionalize power in such a way as to allay these tensions. If they did not do so, because of a false dream of a completely harmonious spontaneity and of a community without power or structure, they would undoubtedly end up with the opposite result: the absolute power of the strongest. Indeed, in contrast, between the strong and the weak, the institutionalization of power—the law—frees, while liberty oppresses. A community without structure quickly becomes a place where the domination of those with the loudest voices asserts itself. Even the most allegedly spontaneous prayer groups often develop a subtle and discreet organization of power which prevents the most extroverted from imposing their will excessively on the others. Institutional structures are necessary for a certain order.

Indispensable as they are, institutions nonetheless remain places of oppression. The well-known contradiction of institutions lies in the fact that they are both necessary and oppressive. The Bible refers to this ambivalence in the different stories about the establishment of royalty in Israel. The king is the one who guides the people and protects the widow and orphan; but he is also the one who levies taxes, imposes conscription, and makes slaves of the population.

In all societies, rites promote an approach to the societal tensions connected with organizational structures. And, as power is both fascinating and frightening, such rites will be sacralized more than others; this is typically shown in the sacrament of ordination.

The ideologies which give legitimacy to power are generally ideologies of service; but few people harbor any illusions: In practice, power is always partly oppression. Christians, too, have to confront this question. The gospel does so in various places and the whole story of the passion speaks of it. The most explicit text on this point is perhaps that in which Jesus urges those who have power in Christian communities not to be like those who wield it in the rest of society: "Let them be truly servants and not masters in disguise." The passion itself shows how he who was of divine condition washed the feet of his friends and died rejected. These stories contain a whole philosophy of power.

The ministries

Christian traditions view the institutions of power in the form of a multiplicity of services (ministries) with which a community provides itself. The service that is essential to the community is, by definition, however, incapable of being institutionalized. We are speaking of the charisma of prophecy, that is, the charisma of those who by their words and symbolic or concrete acts will impart dynamism to the community and reveal to it God's word today. Such charisma cannot be institutionalized because the Spirit springs from everywhere spontaneously in the community. It would make no sense to attribute this gift to any particular people; the Spirit of God blows where it wishes and no one can determine whence it will come nor whither it will go. The instituted ministries—those which have been called orders in the church—are therefore not the most important; their particular feature is simply to be linked to the organization and division of powers in the community. This raises the question of how Christian communities were traditionally organized.

Historians seem to be increasingly sure that, right at the start, Christian communities did not possess an episcopal ministry of the sort we know today. A community lived, animated by a number of prophetic voices, and "elders" settled the questions that arose. Some communities also set up a sort of executive secretary, a type of "supervisor" (a bishop); and, as often happens in groups, the power of the one who fulfilled this role increased to such an extent that fairly soon it was said that all power in the community flowed from him. Moreover, as could be expected (for ordinary human, not evangelical reasons), the structures of the church copied those of society.

The church and its ministers

On the eve of the Second Vatican Council, the Christian communities conveyed two pictures of the church. Each of them saw in Jesus the total gift of the Father; but after that point they diverged. One offered a pyramidal structure: Jesus giving his power to the pope and bishops, who delegated part of this power to the priests, who watched over the people of God. This conception was rejected by the greater part of the council in favor of another, whereby Jesus gives salvation immediately to the whole of the people of God, the church. The latter as a whole bears witness to the faith of the apostles, offers the eucharistic sacrifice to the Father, teaches the Good News and lives the various sacramental celebrations. The whole church is both teaching and taught. In this church services or ministries are performed, for example, those of bishops, pope, priests, deacons, theologians, catechists, etc.; all in their way serve the people of God and help it to be collectively the "sacrament of salvation," that is, the visibility of the Good News of God's love announced in Jesus. This portrayal makes it possible to distinguish certain functions of the entire church, on the one hand, and of particular ministries, on the other. Thus, it is for the *entire* church to teach the apostolic faith and to speak with authority, that is to say, to exercise a "magisterium." The bishops, for their part, have a special ministry with respect to this task. They are not the whole teaching church; they are its servants.

From the same historical perspective, it is important to note that at the beginning Christian communities had no ministers resembling our present priests, in the worship sense of the word (in Greek: a *hiereus*). The *presbuteroi* were the elders, but the idea of a priest as a man of worship, an attendant of the temple, and mediator between God and people does not seem to have been that of the early churches. The true adoration took place neither in the temple or on Mount Garizim but in spirit and in truth. The tradition has, moreover, been preserved that it was the *whole* church community which celebrated the Eucharist and which (when this idea assumed meaning) "consecrated," under the presidency of the bishop or a priest. Moreover, up to the Middle Ages the tradition was forcefully maintained that one could not legitimately give "orders" to anyone except when a community had need of his or her services. The concept of a priest having powers (almost magical), aside from the community which he serves, ordained in an absolute manner, that is, without a link with a community, and *afterwards* receiving jurisdiction to serve a specified community, is a much later idea which is open to discussion.

In short, the historical research and theological developments which followed Vatican II seem to show that it is the whole community that is primarily the "sacrament of the manifestation of God" and that the people are "priestly." Within the community are constituted a series of ministries which need not necessarily be placed in hierarchical order. Some of these ministries relate to the organization (order) of the community and are instituted. Others, on the other hand, like the charisma of prophecy and perhaps what today is called the religious life, cannot be instituted and organized, on pain of trying to channel the breath of the Spirit. The church cannot "organize" these charismas and ministries; the most it can do is recognize them.

Bishops and priests

Among the ministries instituted, the most important are the episcopate and the presbyterate. According to church traditions, it seems that the episcopate receives a mandate for two particular ministries. The first is connected with organization and government; the pastoral task of the bishops seems to be to animate the people of God and to help the community organize itself to receive the gift of God to the world. The second ministry is connected with the function of the whole church, which is to bear witness to the faith of the apostles. In the case of this ministry, recent theological developments are rather interesting. Before the council, the majority of catholics believed that the role of the bishops was to guard the "deposit of faith" and to bear witness to it in their teaching. Now that the council has given a greater place to the whole of the Christian community, theologians seem to be increasingly stressing the fact that the ministry of the bishops is to "bear witness" to the faith of *their* church with respect to the *universal* church and to the world. Their particular role in bearing witness to the faith of the apostles does not appear to flow from a special light that is not connected with their pastoral function; rather they are asked to bear witness before the universal church to the action of the Spirit which has been revealed in their community. The special insights which are theirs are due to the fact that their ministry causes them to touch the work of the Spirit in their local church.

Similarly, the ministry of the presbyter is perceived in a different way as soon as priority is given to the world and to the whole of the people of God and not to a particular group of ministers. Recent theological developments and historical studies stress the break which Jesus seems to have caused between the Jewish and the Christian priesthood. The former made the priest into a man of sacred things, while the latter tends rather to make him the minister of the community, Christ being the only mediator. From this point of view, the priest receives a commission to rally the church and enable it to fulfill its task. His role appears therefore to be primarily to bring the community together, to signify to it in word and deed that power comes from God alone and that no one can appropriate it, and afterwards to speak in the name of the community (for example, by proclaiming the forgiveness of God and of the community). The power of the priest is not therefore "the power to consecrate" or alone to pronounce God's forgiveness, but to speak on behalf of the community (the church) in order to signify the communion of the whole church which makes real the presence of Christ in the Eucharist and which proclaims the forgiveness of God. If the priest presides over the Eucharist, it is not by virtue of special powers that enable him alone to consecrate, but simply because he is the one who gathers the community together; in this he has the task of revealing the action of Christ who brings together the people of God.

From this point of view, it may be interesting to remember, too, that in the Middle Ages, when one spoke of the "sacrament of ordination," two meanings were intended. The first meaning, similar to what the majority understands today, referred to ordination, that is, to the mandate or mission given. In the second meaning, however, it is the community of priests itself that is the sacrament. It is the college of presbyters itself which is called upon to signify and to make real for Christians the gift of God, which is a liberating power. The very power exercised by the "elders" of the community is called upon to signify the liberating power of God.

How can those who will exercise the ministry of the priesthood in this way be chosen or appointed? First of all, it is undoubtedly important to recognize clearly that this ministry is linked to a community. Ordaining someone as a priest therefore implies that a group needs to have such a minister. It is then necessary to find a person who has the charisma to lead that community, to be its spokesperson and thereby to signify the word of God in its midst. The purpose is not, as happens too often, to ordain someone and then to find a community which they can serve. Rather is it the aim, on the basis of the church's needs, to find people who can render these services and to ordain them (possibly after some specialized training, if this is necessary). This return to the needs of communities will perhaps bring with it a more diversified concept of the ministries. Someone who has the charisma to conduct the celebration of the sacraments does not necessarily have the charisma of leadership for the community's action in society. Or again, someone might be ordained for a teaching ministry without the community recognizing and ratifying in that person the charisma of leadership in worship celebrations. There are many situations in which persons may be called upon to speak in the name of the church and thereby to signify in sacramental fashion the presence of God in God's church; various forms of ordination, possibly temporary, could correspond to these different situations.

Each of these ordinations establishes a bond between that person and the whole church, and thereby modifies the network of relationships defining the person. This is probably the direction in which the explanation must be sought for the theological doctrines that speak of the sacramental character: the idea of "character" would refer to the tissue of relationships which in the end mark and shape the person. In any case, it is obvious that, in traditional theologies, the *person* is the priest, and priesthood is not just a profession. The power of God liberating and bringing together his people cannot be symbolized through an impersonal role. The priesthood is different from a strictly "professional" function, like that of a psychologist who can help his or her patient without being personally involved. The very involvement of the priest as a person is called upon to reveal the liberating God.

In the sacrament of ordination, as in all others, the sacrament, the gift of God, is constituted by the human and historical reality lived in the Christian community. This gift of God is related to the church community. For that reason, certain theologians wonder whether, in the case of a church community wishing to celebrate the Eucharist and no one in its midst being ordained, it could not itself, as an exception, commission (i.e., ordain) someone to preside over its Eucharist. This would not be placing itself outside the apostolic traditions but rather existing as a Christian community, that is, as a eucharistic community.

Ordination: celebration of the tensions of power

Against this background, it becomes possible to see what, among other things, could be expressed by a celebration of the sacrament of ordination.

Such a celebration should first show how the Christian community sees itself as a place where the love of God is revealed. It is that community, the people of God, the "priestly people," that gives thanks to the Father and celebrates the wonders that God accomplishes in his people.

The necessity for ministries in the community could be mentioned; the community must be structured in such a way that all, and particularly the poor and the humble, can contribute to the life and word of the church. It is also necessary for the forgiveness of God to be proclaimed. The specific needs of the local church for which ministers are to be commissioned (i.e., ordained) could be expressed; one does not ordain ministers in a vacuum but in the presence of the particular historical situations of God's people.

The ambiguity of power in the community deserves then to be clearly stated. Readings concerning the ambivalence of royalty in Israel and the recommendation of Christ to the "first among his disciples" not to adopt the habits of the princes of this world may be useful. Here again, this reflection on power cannot remain purely abstract. Power is not felt in the same way in a monarchy, a democracy or a dictatorship, in an urban or rural community, in a unified culture or in a cosmopolitan multiracial society, in an economy in expansion or recession, etc. The reasoning of the community may vary with the situation; for instance, one does not speak in the same way in a clerical church and in a church made up of grassroots communities. In any case, the evangelical message must be proclaimed: In the Christian community, God alone is Father, master and Lord, while all human beings are brothers and sisters. And although master and Lord, God has not wished to keep these titles. On the contrary, in Jesus he made himself brother and friend, remaining content to bear witness to the Father's immense love and revealing it. Jesus did not wish to speak in his own name but to bear witness to his Father and to the work of the Spirit. His authority was not oppressive like that of the scribes and Pharisees; his power was not exercised like that of the occupying army and its collaborators. He came close to the poor, the sinners, the rejected; he defended the humble against the ideological oppression of the law; he refused to be treated like a master and washed the feet of his disciples. He dared to speak with authority when it was necessary to defend the oppressed, to prevent the law from crushing the poor, or to proclaim that the kingdom was open to little ones. This approach to power caused him to be viewed by the Pharisees as subversive and by the people as Good News. For this too, he was eventually rejected, condemned and put to death. In Christ's life, there is a whole philosophy about power.

Power in the Christian community will be a sacrament (that is, an effective manifestation of God's love) insofar as it reflects the "style" of Jesus. In a world where oppressions abound, the celebration of the sacrament of ordination thus leads Christians to remember the eschatological hope of the kingdom where power will be liberating. It also summons priests to exercise, as Jesus did, the power commissioned to them.

A society marked by human oppressions (symbolized in theology as the results of original sin) is far removed from such a way of living power. When the community (the church) appoints one of its own to accomplish certain services in its name, it always has the fear that the person will abuse the power conferred. Nevertheless, seeing a sacrament in priestly ordination, Christian communities place their trust in hope; they dare to look at the problem of power with the hope that the liberating action of God will be revealed in the community's power structures. As it is in the other sacraments, this hope is eschatological, not perfectly realized in the present. It is therefore meaningful for Christian communities to express this ambivalence of power in their midst as one of the situations in which the history of salvation is made. To believe that the story of salvation, the liberation that comes from God, can be found in these ambiguities is, in my view, to hope to find a gift, called the sacrament of ordination, in the structures of power.

In this framework, communities can celebrate the gift of "priestly powers" to individuals who have shown that they possess charisma. As Jesus mentioned to Pilate at the time of his judgment, all power finally comes from God. That means that no one can appropriate power in his or her own name. That is why it is the whole church that—through its spokespersons, the bishops—ordains. In this context, priestly powers are not quasi-magical or sacred powers but instead are linked to the human community, the church.

Thus, the "powers" of the priests, deacons or any other person ordained in the church never belong exclusively to individuals; they belong to the community. The fact that not everyone has equal powers is not because certain people alone possess a personal and semi-magical power but because commissioned ministers are needed to ensure that the rights of God's people are protected. For example, preaching has traditionally been reserved for deacons; the purpose of this, too, is to protect the church from individuals who might assume the right to impose their sermons on the community without having been commissioned for this purpose. No one has the right to impose himself on the church as a leader. Unfortunately, what should have been a protection for the people of God has sometimes been turned against them; this has happened when ordained ministers have monopolized the powers conferred on them and used them for themselves and not for the community. If, for example, the Christian assembly wants someone to preach the word of God to it, it would be an abuse of power on the part of ordained ministers to prevent that person from doing so on the grounds that they and they alone have been ordained for this purpose. On the other hand, when an eccentric wishes to impose his or her sermons, it is quite normal to recall that it is necessary to have been ordained in order to preach. The essential is to see that powers which have been conferred possess a meaning only with respect to the church and not against it.

In short, to be ordained for a ministry is to be empowered to speak and act in the name of the church, with all that this implies, and to be able in this way to make God present in the people. It is to have the responsibility for a power to be exercised in the name of Christ and in his style. For the church, the celebration of ordination is the achievement of this new structuring. In recognizing the new priest as its leader and authorized spokesperson, the community establishes a new organization of powers; this new structure, moreover, transforms the new priest by altering his relationships with the whole of the people of God.

The ministry of the celebrations of the sacraments

Among the important ministries in the church, there is one which has unfortunately lost much of its importance: the ministry of leader of rites linked to the service of the sacraments and celebrations of the church. As the power of a priest has too often been regarded as semi-magical, priests and Christians have lost sight of the meaning of the expression, "conducting a celebration." If a priest is asked to bless an object, it often happens that he feels compelled to give a blessing whose nearly superstitious nature he deplores. Would it not be possible to interpret the request in a completely different way, that is, as an invitation to conduct a celebration through which Christians will be able to recognize that this object, which seems important to them—a house, for example—is a gift of God? And to do that not simply by reciting a form of words or a prayer, but by celebrating together with Christians the gift of God represented by that object? This is more difficult than giving a blessing, the text of which appears in a book; to do so, the priest must conduct a celebration and construct a liturgy which will help Christian men and women better to live the events of their existence. In some cases, prayers will be taken from rituals, but in other situations, if the person conducting the blessing is capable of it, he or she will find words and acts more fitted to the events. The teaching of one of the oldest texts of the church is still relevant: "Let the prophets say the eucharistic prayer as they wish" (*Didache,* 10,7). The same rule applies to all the sacraments; too often they have been made into formal rites rather than celebrations which must be led so as to make them meaningful and powerful experiences.

This rigid formulation of the sacraments and of other "sacramentals" is the reason for the crisis of identity experienced by many parish priests who regret spending their lives celebrating burials, marriages or Eucharists. For them, this is not a true calling, nor a ministry which involves their personalities and know-how. They often find greater pleasure in other services such as individual guidance or the organization of parish functions; there at least they have the impression of affecting people's lives. This way of seeing things is reflected in their training; one would not dare, for example, to launch a priest into the ministry without giving him at least basic training in pastoral counseling. However, for the very difficult art which involves the conduct of rites and celebrations and assistance to the community to come into contact with its contradictions, conflicts and other deep-lying feelings, effective training is seldom provided. "Liturgical" training is often provided, but it rarely makes people able to lead and structure a celebration. This requires a multi-disciplinary approach which should include the following subjects: introduction to group dynamics, the theory of the effectiveness of rites, perception of societal and theological dimensions, and the acquisition of awareness concerning the place of words and of the body. This actually is more difficult than providing guidance. Moreover, if we had better leaders of rites who effectively helped people to express and explore the tensions of their experience, we would less often find it necessary to resort to the techniques of individual psychology. It is a characteristic of a society of private individuals to have almost completely eliminated the vocation of leader of rites, and to have replaced it by that of counselors. Nevertheless, the rite often better respects the autonomy of individuals and groups than psychological techniques. This is not to deprecate the art of psychotherapy but rather to upgrade that of leaders of rites.

Might not one of the reasons of the semi-failure of the liturgical renewal be that it has provided priests with courses in liturgy but has not helped them to express in renewed sacramental rites the history of the people? If the vocation of leader of rites were given greater importance and better preparation, parish priests would feel more useful because they would have a better way of approaching individuals and communities. All celebrations could become what they should be—places where people can make contact, in a communal way, with their own life and feelings; in short, where they can make their own history. For Christian men and women, moreover, this history has a particular name: the history of salvation, that of the liberation that comes from God.

9 | Sacrament of the Sick: Confrontation With Disease and Death

The attitude of our society toward death is ambiguous. We have seen that, some 15 years ago in an economically expanding society, little mention was made of death. The prevailing thought referred to the scientific and technical progress which was going to delay, if not abolish, that event. People are less and less often present at the death of their relatives. A few centuries ago, in a group of 20-year-old students, most of them would already have seen the death of a number of brothers and sisters; the majority would lack one parent, if not both. Today, one frequently meets people of 40 years of age who have not yet lost any of their relatives. It is therefore not surprising that the experience of separation through death is becoming increasingly vague in collective sensitivities. As young adults no longer live with old people, all that relates to the approach of death and the feeling of contemplating the end of one's life is ignored because, quite simply, it is unknown.

The progress of scientific and technological medicine is leading to a view of death as a problem to be solved rather than as a human experience to be lived. We are a long way from those civilizations in which individuals feel the approach of death, can predict the moment of its coming, and await it in the company of their relatives. Medical techniques make it difficult to predict the very moment of death; sometimes the dying person is called back to existence for several days or weeks. These false exits are not without their effects on family and friends and on the ill person. How can people live an imminent separation which keeps on being delayed?

In a technological society as rational as ours, death is difficult to accept; something that cannot be manipulated seems irrational and therefore a scandal. Doctors often try, by almost every means, to continue the struggle against disease, sometimes even when it has become useless or even inhuman. As long as one has something to *do* the irrational and the inevitable can be, to some extent, overshadowed. Those dying people connected to so many instruments that they almost look like laboratories are a symbol: that of a society which wishes to control everything by technology. My intention is not, of course, to deny the benefits of medicine, which sometimes succeeds, through intensive care, in saving a patient; I am speaking only of the symbolic meanings of certain forms of misplaced therapeutic zeal. The tendency, nowadays happily fading out, to put dying people in the hospital and to take them away from their familiar background may perhaps be part of this attempt to expel death. One has the impression that our society does not know how to confront death; accordingly, it finds a thousand ways of masking it. Unfortunately the way the sacrament of the sick is sometimes celebrated demonstrates the inability of Christian communities to face and get in touch with death and disease.

In our economically declining society, confidence in technology and the future is melting away, while the fear of death is taking other forms. Some books speak of life after death as if people returned from it; they relate common aspirations and evade the reality of the separations represented by death. In the end, they empty it of all substance and deny it.

The mysterious character of death makes the univocal language of reason inadequate for approaching it. Through it, nevertheless, human beings are confronted with the ultimate meanings of their existence. As in other situations overloaded with meanings, only a ritual, symbolic, plurisignificant language is appropriate here. It must supply forms of expression which support the feelings of the participants without enclosing them within the boundaries of an overly precise language. It was probably wrong to disparage those vigils at the bedside of a sick person at which, for example, the participants recited the rosary. It is true that these forms of prayer lose their meaning when they are used simply to fill a gap in communication, or when they are used specifically to avoid communication, or when they become magical. Traditionally, however, this manner of praying doubtless worked differently; saying the rosary became a form of communal communication when one knew that there was no longer anything specific to communicate. When one had said everything one wished to say, instead of remaining in silence, the rosary allowed an expression in which all felt themselves in communion. Where a community feels itself in union of thought, a very simple and ritualized prayer can convey very diverse feelings which it is sometimes better not to try to express clearly. The persons who conducted these prayer vigils often had a sense of what should be said and done in order that through these rituals each person might get in touch with what he or she was living. Unfortunately, with the passing of time, prayers were said *for* the dying persons or *for* their recovery, or their salvation, instead of being a simple living together of the mystery which had assembled a community. More than ever, our society must rediscover ritual actions in order to aid the patient and the community to live all that comes before them in these circumstances.

Celebrating the confrontation with disease and death

The sacrament of the sick should be designed to help the sick person and his or her relatives to get in touch with their feelings and to discover, in disease and death themselves, a gift and a hope coming from God. For this to be possible, a series of objectives can be assigned to the celebration. I shall mention five: to succeed in speaking serenely of death and disease; to live together the trial and human reality of imminent separation; to discover the new freedom which can be lived by those who are approaching death, in particular, the freedom which allows people to forgive one another and even to be reconciled; to approach with the greatest possible tranquillity everything that remains as a kind of "unfinished business" in a person's life; to live the end of a life together in hope, remembering the death of Jesus.

Speaking serenely of disease and death

Many are afraid in the face of death, particularly in our scientific and technological culture; its mystery is such that our rational culture often mounts a conspiracy of silence with regard to the dying person. Unfortunately one often meets situations in which everyone avoids mentioning death, although everyone has it constantly in mind. The dying person will confide to distant friends that he is not deceived but that he is playing out the story of recovery because he does not wish to cause pain to his relatives. The latter, in the meantime, ask everyone to make sure that the dying person is not allowed to guess the seriousness of his condition, "because it would be too painful for him."

The celebration of the sacrament of the sick can help the community to confront the anxiety connected with death. For this to happen, the sacrament should evoke with warmth and empathy the feelings generally linked with the process of accepting an irreparable loss. These feelings have been described by many psychologists, among them, E. Kubler Ross.[1]

An initial reaction is often to deny reality: Even if one has all the information, one cannot or (unconsciously) one does not want to see. The case of the cancer specialist being treated in a cancer ward is often mentioned. All the symptoms and treatments of his disease are familiar to him but he is incapable of recognizing his condition. The patient at this stage tends to isolate himself and to reject reality.

A second stage (not so separate in actual experience) reveals in the patient (and sometimes in his or her family and friends) irritation in the face of the seriousness of the situation. After all, it is reasonable to feel anger and frustration when one is seriously or incurably ill.

1. *On Death and Dying,* New York, N.Y.: Macmillan, 1969.

Then, many dying people try to "bargain" with their destiny. They are ready to accept death, but they try to see if destiny cannot be accommodated so as to lighten the loss. They act rather like those people who perceive that, despite their wishes, they will not be able to be in two places at the same time; they use mental gymnastics to try to reconcile the irreconcilable. The same applies when death is being faced; many people attempt to see how they can both accept death and not leave a whole series of undertakings unfinished.

Amid these processes, anger, denial, bargaining and periods of depression alternate. In the best cases, patients eventually move toward an acceptance of their death; they then find it possible to live it with serenity and hope.

A good celebration must enable all these feelings to come to the surface. The leader of the rite must try to create conditions such that all the participants feel accepted with their fears, rejections, denials, isolations, irritations, bargainings, depressions and, finally, their acceptance and hope. The art of the person who conducts the celebration consists in symbolically reflecting the feelings present in the community, without forcing the process of confrontation with death but also without denying it. While refraining from reducing the sacrament to a simple group therapy in the face of death, it must be acknowledged that a good celebration can accomplish some of the purposes of such therapy. The sacrament helps people to approach death or to confront disease together, as a community; it makes it possible to share some of the feelings involved and sometimes to come to a certain peace.

Face to face with imminent separation and loss

Disease and death involve separation and loss, which are the cause of many sufferings. A few centuries ago our Western culture was more capable of confronting these. A person about to die called his relatives to his bedside and bade them farewell; the French word "adieu" (i.e., to God, meaning "farewell") is appropriate because it expresses the idea that life is, in the end, abandoned to the ultimate, to God, in openness to the future. Acceptance of the loss of one's life, and of one's friends and goods, however, is not easy either for the dying person or for the relatives. The celebration may be an excellent moment for getting in touch with some of the feelings experienced in the face of these separations. There again, the many meanings of ritual words and acts sometimes make it possible to approach realities which would overwhelm one's sensitivities if these same realities were referred to directly and rationally.

The freedom of those who face death

Human beings always have something to defend, if only their lives. In the face of death, at least when accepted, a person has less to preserve and becomes more free. The human interests that one has defended during life lose part of their importance; certain values are seen from a new standpoint. The dying thus bring a new truth to our human lives. How many times, before the finality of death, have people taken important steps, for example, in the direction of forgiveness and reconciliation? People who no longer have anything to defend (provided this is true, for there are also dying people who carry out a certain type of blackmail!) have an uncommon capacity to break through the armor of human defenses. That is why those who live this trial must have, in the celebration, the possibility of expressing themselves. This can be done very simply, for example, by asking the sick person to give a blessing to all the persons present, either in a group or, in some cases, to individuals. Such a prayer has a particular meaning since it comes from someone who is no longer subject to the tensions of our production-oriented society, from a sick person who therefore cannot justify his or her existence or words by work or efficiency; it is the word of someone who depends and receives. It matters that such persons be allowed to speak, if only to say thank you to those who are caring for them. Too often in our society, sick people are reduced to the role of "patients," that is, people who only endure. To counteract this tendency, the sick must be allowed to speak. It is good for the community to listen to the message of someone who, if people are reduced to cost-effective terms, is almost nothing. The freedom and the words of the sick, who live by receiving in trust, are a special gift of God.

Confronting what will never be finished

In the face of death, one of the most significant trials is the failure to complete what one would have liked: educating a child, seeing a loved one again, finishing a task, being reconciled with an enemy or, simply, living until the first communion or marriage of a child or grandchild. At the moment of death, some of these projects will generally remain unfinished. The celebration of the sacrament of the sick may be an important moment, helping the community and the dying to leave these tasks in the hands of God. Perhaps some of them will be achieved before the end, while others will remain uncompleted.

Disease may also add new relational problems due, among other things, to the tensions and aggression which it may trigger both in the patient and in the patient's immediate circle of family and friends. These difficulties result in wounds that will not be healed because time is too short. This is another tangible boundary represented by death; even after the most sincere of reconciliations, new clashes do not fail to occur.

The celebration itself can help some of these shortcomings to be lived and, sometimes, to be resolved. For instance, I remember a case where, in a hospital bedroom, a sick woman agreed to entrust to God the sorrow caused to her by her divorce and remarriage; a family reconciliation took place and, as if by some sort of miracle, a series of family difficulties were eased because, in the face of death, all these problems were considered from a different viewpoint. Time may sometimes work very quickly at the end of a life; good celebrations can help to give such times their fullness.

Living the end of life together

At the end of an existence, memories of events and persons are laden with special meanings. One remembers all those who lived and who, by their lives, have enabled existence to be meaningful. To illustrate this point, let us consider a story which will convey more than any theory.

An old woman who lived in a slum had enjoyed for several years celebrating the Christmas Eve Eucharist with a small group in her home. Gently but firmly she had always refused to be put in a nursing home. There was some doubt as to whether she would live until Christmas. A friend said, "She will certainly last until then because she is determined to celebrate Christmas. But she won't last for long afterwards."

During the eucharistic celebration she related her life, youth, trials, loneliness, joys. Then the whole community remembered Jesus, his last evening when he too had reviewed his life, had placed his trust in the Father, and looked ahead to his death. The celebration had spoken both of the life of that old person and of that of Jesus; it had also evoked their deaths. The eucharistic words: "Here is my body, here is my life," assumed their full meaning at the end of this woman's life. The following evening, neighbors found the old lady dead.

In the passion and death of Jesus, Christian traditions have always found the inspiration and comfort needed to live the end of existence. Jesus is not called upon as the magic solution to all tension, but the story of his trust in the face of death can enlighten communities concerning what they are living; hearing his story, Christian communities have tried to face the reality of their death. Christians try to go beyond those superficial stories which mention death only in the form of a transition, as if the loss of life was not real and as if the mysterious affirmation of the resurrection was a way to elude the confrontation with the meaninglessness of death. Jesus experienced this meaninglessness in the evening of his life, and in that framework he delivered up his Spirit to his Father. His resurrection does not resolve all the questions with which death confronts human beings; but Christians have always felt that, in the footsteps of Jesus, there was a meaning in facing death and even in living it with hope. The account of the attitude of Jesus in the face of his death is not a solution to the questions raised by that death; and yet it helps us to embark, in his wake, upon the unknown of the beyond. Finally, the proclamation of the resurrection of Jesus and of the promise of resurrection for each and every person is a mysterious assertion which is important to recognize. Although it is necessary to avoid using the promise of resurrection to deny the reality of death, it states forcefully that life must not be reduced to its superficial appearances and that to God nothing is impossible.

A sacrament to be celebrated with sensitivity

Even more than the other sacraments, the rite of the sick requires the celebrant to display finesse; it must be celebrated differently depending on what is being experienced by the sick person and the community. It is fortunate that the sacrament has a sign fixed once and for all: unction. This is a stable symbolic element around which the celebration can be focused and adapted according to needs, in order to find the words, actions and movements which will subsequently enable the community and the sick person to say: "We are better able to confront disease, old age, death, separation and to live all this together, remembering the passion of Jesus; in this sacrament, the gift of God has revealed itself anew."

Funerals

As a result of the historical development of sacramental structures, it happens that funerals are not a sacrament. They are, nonetheless, the moment when the Christian community expresses what it experiences at the separation of the loved one. Funerals are perverted when they become a negation of death and separation, and when these realities are denied in the name of the resurrection.

For funerals to be meaningful, it is important that the community should be able to *live its mourning*. In the face of death, it will also pass through all the stages described above: denials, refusal to see the reality and consequences of death, fear of new situations, anger in the face of death, bargaining which refuses to consider what will change in existence, depression, and the beginnings of acceptance and hope. If well celebrated, funerals can help people to get in touch with these feelings, to remember the departed one, and to live the separation. In this framework there will be a meaning in proclaiming, without attempting to deny how mysterious this proclamation is, what Christian communities have also felt to be the center of their faith: Jesus is alive and he is the life of the world.

10 | Conclusion: Let the Sacraments Be

Taking everything into account, in the face of sociological and phenomenological assessments, the sacraments are not doing too badly. The seven sacraments even appear as a good basis for analyzing the main tensions of existence: welcome and hope in the presence of new life, the risk of decisions, acquisition of a say in matters and the acceptance of responsibility, conflicts and forgiveness, power, the family and, finally, the trial of disease and death. In all these "passages" faith discovers the gracious gift of God and the hope of the liberation of men and women. This is what sacramental rites delve into and celebrate in the church.

The analysis which I have given obviously does not provide a complete view of what may be experienced in these celebrations; depending on cultures, the histories of communities and individuals, the various developments and the conflicts of societies, other riches of Christian symbolism may be manifested, recalled, discovered or created. Undoubtedly the important thing is to believe in the possibilities and the dynamic of these traditions; symbols must be allowed to *live*. To "let the sacraments be" means allowing a proliferation of different traditions which will reveal depths unknown to psychosociological management techniques or to those moralizing celebrations whose principal aim is to adapt individuals to the group. It also means refusing to allow previous formulations to block the

155

dynamism of the gospel. Traditions are lived only by risk-
ing them, that is, by actualizing them, and therefore
developing and transforming them. I have indicated,
moreover, how rites are always the object of "transactions" which revitalize them. Finally, and above all, to
"let the sacraments be" means, through them, to get in
touch with the conflicts and contradictions of our societies
and our individual lives. At the center of Christian traditions concerning the sacraments a triple dimension is
found: confrontation with the gratuitousness of the gift of
God, confrontation with evil and injustice, and hope of a
global liberation.

Will a better understanding and a rediscovery of these
dimensions be sufficient to bring about a renewal of ritual
practices in a church marked by scientific and technological rationality? Will they, for example, enable parishes to
revive Christian "feasts" and to discover in them how the
strength of the gospel is revealed? Undoubtedly no! A
renaissance of symbolism in society cannot come about
through intellectual research alone. Nor will a simple
liturgical renewal be any more effective; such a renewal is
liable to become a way of bringing people into line.

As celebrations are acts of community, it is first
necessary to concentrate on building communities. To be
firmly based, these will have to have roots (clearly chosen
social solidarities and shared symbols) and causes (for
which they are ready to pay the price); finally, these communities will have to be ready to face—in faith, trust and
by means of exact analyses—their individual and social
contradictions and their existential tensions. There lies, in
my view, the basis of any sacramental renewal.

Furthermore, it is necessary for such communities to
understand that they cannot exist as community without
celebrating together what they live. However, this cannot
be done primarily on the basis of intellectual developments
like those that form the pattern of this book. One learns
how living and successful celebrations work only by living
them and not by merely studying them. In order to help
people to become open to this symbolic dimension of
human existence, it is necessary to train leaders of rites

who can bring about celebrations that are in touch with what is lived.

To me, these conditions appear necessary for the symbolic universe described in this book to be alive. A true sacramental renewal should not only allow the sacraments to be but should also open up a symbolic side in our one-dimensional society; it is, indeed, the world and society in its entirety that is the goal of the salvation offered to us in Jesus Christ.

Appendix:
Celebrations,
Conflicts,
Tenderness

I will synthesize here some ideas which have been present throughout the book regarding how to celebrate in the midst of the conflicts of life. These reflections respond to the following questions about the celebration of sacraments: Is it possible to celebrate Jesus Christ in a community whose members have diverse and often conflicting interests, and opposite views on social issues? How can such a celebration be authentic and relevant for everyone present? Are conflicts themes at the core of a Christian celebration or obstacles to be removed before celebrating? Do power relationships affect a celebration? Does the authority of the presider infringe on the freedom of the participants in a liturgy? How is space provided for freedom in a spontaneous celebration? With whom is it meaningful to celebrate? Can it be with anybody or should some people be excluded? Who is excluded? Is there some violence involved in any celebration? Should people leave celebrations with more peace in their hearts? What does that mean? Do symbols manipulate people in a celebration?

a. In the background of every celebration are societal relationships filled with contradictions, conflicts and oppressions. When they engage in celebrations, people are always affected by their situation as individuals and as members of particular groups or social classes. I suggest that it is helpful to distinguish two main perspectives. In the first one, people believe that there is no problem, either in the community, in society, or among individuals. As some say: "In the world, you're OK, and I'm OK, and that is it." Others say: "Deep down, we all agree; so let us forget our differences and let us celebrate together." That means that practically all tensions are dismissed, with the result of a feeling of unreality. Everybody knows what it means to hear someone say, "Deep down, we agree," when conflicts are very much present. When that is the case, celebration often becomes mere diversion or superficial entertainment.

In the second perspective, people recognize that there are tensions, contradictions and conflicts. A wedding, for example, celebrates not only the joy of a new and blossoming love, but also the tension and suffering of parents who realize that their children are leaving them. In another example, when some people celebrate work, others remain unemployed. Or, the joy of somebody coming back safe from war does not take away the anguish of continuing wars. So-called spontaneous celebrations of life can sometimes actually give privileges to those who enjoy more "culture" or those who speak easily or those who can entertain. If, in a celebration, we truly want to listen to what teen-agers have to say, we still often manage to manipulate them. A birthday celebration does not suppress all the tensions in a family. At the celebration for the opening of a new library, the workers who built it are not always invited. When a priest is ordained to serve the Christian community, he is a male in a church dominated by males. Each of these examples shows how in the background of every celebration, or of every event to be celebrated, there are conflicts, tensions and contradictions that have to be taken into account. At the root of all of this is some expression of the evil present in the world. In theological terms, which are also related to anthropological analysis, I would speak of the sin of the world or of the results of original sin, i.e., structural evil in history. It is in recognizing these hard realities that celebrations are meaningful. If they are denied, what remains will seem empty, superficial and inauthentic.

b. Every celebration divides and excludes. Every celebration stems from a particular culture and social group. No celebration belongs to anyone and everyone. In a unity marked by tensions and filled with oppression and contradictions, a celebration divides people, even if every participant dreams of a world without division. (Such a "kingdom" does not belong to our world except in hope and through some partial realizations. Sometimes we can glimpse it through acting it out, with the hope that the imitation will give us the foretaste of such a kingdom.) So every celebration excludes people, even if those who organize it wish to welcome everybody. A Christian celebration turns off those who do not want to have anything to do with Jesus Christ. The celebration of the struggle of the workers excludes the managers, unless they choose to be in solidarity with the workers. A celebration to get in touch with what happens when a factory is closed will exclude the representative of the multinational that decided to move the plant elsewhere. The celebration of those who want to stop thinking of an economic depression will exclude those who want to celebrate their solidarity with the unemployed. A wedding of young people who want to celebrate according to their taste will partly exclude their parents and grandparents. Even the feast of love (making love) excludes others. When Jesus ate with the publicans and the sinners, he so separated himself from the Pharisees. Finally, there always is the exclusion of those who prefer not to celebrate.

Every celebration thus excludes, even if people do not intend that, or if they desire to have a universal celebration. Exclusion can be experienced even more when those in authority attempt to conceal the reality by statements such as: "Let us forget our divisions and celebrate."

But if every celebration excludes some, does it make any sense to go on a guilt trip because of these exclusions, or would it be more appropriate to recognize and reflect on the community of interest that is present or absent in the celebration?

c. Every celebration is instituted by some, and involves some power and some violence. It can be oppressive. When individuals or groups initiate a celebration (i.e., institute it), they assume some social power. In the process of instituting a celebration, there is always some violence, even if it is not physical. Instituting a celebration means involving people in rites, "games" and processes they do not master. At the end of a feast, people can feel quite happy with what happened, but some can also feel crushed by it. This can be illustrated by some examples. Those who institute a celebration to get in touch with some sociopolitical dimension are imposing their view. On the other hand, those who institute a festive celebration also impose an attitude and an implied content. The celebration of love (relational and/or physical love) also implies some kind of aggression of one desire on the other (people can be quite happy about this, or feel violated). Similarly, the way some decide to celebrate always implies a subtle power play between those who want to celebrate and those who do not.

Many questions can be asked when considering these power plays: Who will institute the celebration? Whose celebration will it be? Who will organize it and chair it? These questions cannot be avoided in the name of freedom, of creativeness for all, and of total spontaneity because that would amount to giving all the power to the person with the most say or the most dominant personality. Power is thus always an issue with respect to the celebration. Power is not the problem, but the risk of oppression is. It is thus proper that every community ask itself how to regulate power and authority in celebrations. But as it is unavoidable that some will have power in the celebration, the question is not to feel guilty about it, but to acknowledge and reflect critically on the way power is handled and on the common interests involved.

d. Every celebration implies some partisan ideology. Some examples will be enough to show that every celebration refers to particular social myths or stories which motivate people and justify some attitudes and actions, while always concealing other issues, at least so far as these stories do not confess how partial they are.

The reading of certain psalms in a celebration can be

touchy because they promote a particular social understanding of the world. Similarly, when people celebrate a person's retiring, that celebration obviously will carry some ideology about what work is. In a liturgy speaking of the solidarity of Jesus with oppressed people, there is also a particular ideological vision. It would be the same in a prayer which stresses individual salvation. In a civil rights protest march, the ideological content is obvious. But any wedding will also promote some social ideas about what a couple, a family and love are. A welcoming celebration for a newborn child will also express how people envision a society which would foster life for this child. The salute to the flag also carries plenty of ideological meanings.

Whatever the celebration or prayer, it will always have some ideological content. The issue is not to induce guilt because of it, but to question the kind of ideologies our celebrations foster.

e. Each celebration involves some obscurity. A celebration acts out and reveals certain realities. But, at the same time, rituals—like ideologies—always involve some obscurity. They conceal some aspects of life. A ritual or a symbol is like a blank page, anyone can put into it almost any meaning, concealing many disparities. (Just think of the many meanings that can be invested in a birthday cake.) There is only one thing you can be sure of in a celebration: It will hide many differences. It will also make people aware of differences, even if only in a preconscious way. The best way to ruin a celebration is to insist that it have the same meaning for everyone. That is why, even when nobody wants to confuse anybody, a celebration, by its very nature, is always mystifying. There does not exist such a thing as a pure, transparent and unambiguous celebration. Even the expression, "We are all so happy together and we all understand one another!" contributes to the ambiguity of a situation by not recognizing the limits of what is shared.

Some mystification—with all its ambiguity—is part of life. It should then not be called bad. It can even be useful to realize that the fear of ambiguities grips the powerful more than the weak who know better how to live with the ambiguities of life.

f. A celebration can also be perverted. Perversion is more than mystification. I call a celebration perverted when it does the contrary of what it says it does. Some examples: a celebration for a hated manager; "making love" without love; a "popular" feast organized by those in power to manipulate people; a Judas' kiss; a Christian celebration (which should express the gratuitous, liberating, and unconditional love of God) which becomes moralizing; a celebration around a dying person in which everyone is careful to avoid any mention of what that person is experiencing because of fear of death.

g. To celebrate in the midst of ambiguities and with tenderness. Considering all that has been said above, people may wonder if it is possible to live any authentic celebration. I believe there is no meaning in trying to have an absolutely "pure" celebration. That is why those who want to follow the motto "No celebration without justice" could find themselves in a deadlock. If people have to wait until justice is established to begin to celebrate, they will never do it. The poor and the oppressed know that well, and they celebrate when they can. But often it is a demand of the privileged ones to have justice and a good conscience. Rather than look for such an ambiguous purity, I would suggest promoting celebrations which get in touch with the contradictions of life. For example, in a feast organized when a child becomes a teen-ager, it is meaningful to express the fears of both the adults and the young in the conflict between the generations. In the celebration for the appointment of a leader, the ambiguities involved in the exercise of power should be acknowledged. In a celebration for victory, the risk of becoming an oppressor should be recognized. In a celebration for the achievement of some task (the harvest or a workshop, for example), the limitations of what has been done, as well as those who have been hurt or diminished in some way by that work, should be mentioned. I submit the following criterion: A celebration becomes more deeply authentic when it does not conceal too much the tensions, contradictions and conflicts connected with what is celebrated, but on the contrary helps us to get in touch with them. Therefore, it is very important to admit, to "confess," the ambiguities that are a part of the celebration, as can be seen in the difference between the publican who confesses his contradictions and the Pharisee who conceals them. Celebrations which hide the contradictions or those which avoid confessing them are often experienced as empty. They become a kind of superficial entertainment or even a farce. As one of my friends once said, "A celebration without a commitment in society soon becomes a farce, but a commitment without celebration becomes deadly boring." Do not some of the difficulties in our celebrations stem from our tendency to conceal our conflicts and our ambiguities?

To face ambiguities, however, the community that celebrates its tensions and conflicts needs a lot of tenderness. Without tenderness and forgiveness such a confrontation becomes unbearable and inhuman and the celebration superficial, empty, alienating, or an opium for the people.

To conclude, here is a criterion of authenticity for celebrations. Celebrations are meant to get people in touch with the deepest realities of their lives, even to the conflicts, contradictions, tensions and oppressions which are always there (whether they are individual or collective). Then, and only then, will people come out of celebrations in peace, as did the publican of the parable. Otherwise, celebrations are distorted (which is in the interest of those who want, consciously or not, to use them to conceal their domination of others and have it legitimated).

hope   p. 110, 111

prophets p. 105

tenderness of forgiveness p. 114
transgressions p. 98 ff
appendix!